The Talmud
of the
Land of Israel

Chicago Studies in the History of Judaism
Edited by
Jacob Neusner
William Scott Green
Calvin Goldscheider

The University of Chicago Press
Chicago and London

The Talmud
of the
Land of Israel

*A Preliminary
Translation and
Explanation*

Volume 17   Sukkah

Translated by
Jacob Neusner

Jacob Neusner is University Professor and the Unger-
leider Distinguished Scholar of Judaic Studies at Brown
University. In addition to editing and translating the
35-volume series *The Talmud of the Land of Israel*, he
is the author of many books, including *Judaism: The
Evidence of the Mishnah* and *Judaism in Society:
The Evidence of the Yerushalmi*, published by the University of Chicago Press.

The University of Chicago Press, Chicago 60637
The University of Chicago Press, Ltd., London

© 1988 by The University of Chicago
All rights reserved. Published 1988
Printed in the United States of America

97 96 95 94 93 92 91 90 89 88   54321

Library of Congress Cataloging-in-Publication Data

Talmud Yerushalmi.   Sukkah.   English.
  Sukkah : a preliminary translation and explanation.

  (Chicago studies in the history of Judaism) (The
Talmud of the land of Israel; v. 17)
    Bibliography: p.
    Includes index.
    1. Talmud Yerushalmi.   Sukkah—Commentaries.
I. Neusner, Jacob, 1932–   . II. Title. III. Series.
IV. Series: Talmud Yerushalmi.   English.   1982; v. 17.
BM498.5.E5   1982 vol. 17   296.1'2407 s   87-13627
[BM506.S9E5]   [296.1'24]
ISBN 0-226-57676-0

For
Alan and Sadie Crown
in friendship

Contents

Foreword

This translation into English of the Talmud of the Land of Israel ("Palestinian Talmud," "Yerushalmi") is preliminary and provisional, even though it is not apt to be replaced for some time. It is preliminary, first, because a firm and final text for translation is not in hand; second, because a modern commentary of a philological and *halakhic* character is not yet available; and, third, because even the lower criticism of the text has yet to be undertaken. Consequently, the meanings imputed to the Hebrew and Aramaic words and the sense ascribed to them in this translation are at best merely a first step. When a systematic effort at the lower criticism of the extant text has been completed, a complete philological study and modern dictionary along comparative lines made available, and a commentary based on both accomplished, then the present work will fall away, having served for the interim. Unhappily, as I said, that interim is apt to be protracted. Text-critics, lexicographers, and exegetes are not apt to complete their work on Yerushalmi within this century.

The purpose of this preliminary translation is to make possible a set of historical and religions-historical studies on the formation of Judaism in the Land of Israel from the closure of the Mishnah to the completion of the Talmud of the Land of Israel and the time of the composition of the first *midrashic* compilations. Clearly, no historical, let alone religions-historical, work can be contemplated without a theory of the principal document and source for the study, the Palestinian Talmud. No theory can be attempted, however tentative and provisional, without a complete, prior statement of what the document appears to wish to say and how its materials seem to have come to closure. It follows that the natural next steps, beyond my now-finished history of Mishnaic law and account of the Judaism revealed in that history, carry us to the present project. Even those steps, when they are taken, will have to be charted with all due regard to the pitfalls of a translation which is preliminary, based upon a text which as yet has not been subjected even to the clarifying exercises of lower criticism. Questions will have to be shaped appropriate to the parlous state of the evidence. But even if the historical and religions-historical program were to be undertaken in the Hebrew language, instead of in English, those who might wish to carry on inquiries into the history of the Jews and of Judaism in the Land of Israel in the third and fourth centuries would face precisely the same task we do. No one can proceed without a systematic account of the evidence and a theory of how the evidence may, and may not, be utilized. Further explanation of the plan and execution of this work will be found at volume 34, pages viii–xii. The glossary, abbreviations, and bibliography, covering the whole, are at volume 34, pages 225–31.

It remains only to thank those who helped with this volume.

My student, Mr. Louis Newman, checked my translation against the Leiden Manuscript and the *editio princeps*, V, and saved me a great deal of tedious work in so doing. He also uncovered more than a few points requiring attention and correction. I am grateful for his hard and careful work. Professor Irving Mandelbaum, of the University of Texas, served as the critical reader for this volume. I am thankful for the many corrections and observations supplied by him and, still more, for his willingness to take time out to study this tractate and so improve my work on it. I retain full responsibility for whatever unsolved problems and deficiencies may remain.

My student, Mr. Roger Brooks, looked up all the biblical verses in this tractate, saving me much work. Miss Winifred Bell typed them. Mrs. Marie Louise Murray typed the entire manuscript and did so with unusual care and a high standard of accuracy. She also contributed corrections of various details. I could not have done this work without the help of these loyal co-workers.

Introduction to Sukkah

This brief tractate supplies further information about objects and rites defined by Scripture's commandments for *the Festival*, Mishnah's name for Sukkot, the feast of booths. Since it is Scripture which lays matters out, we have now to consider the relevant verses:

Lev. 23:33–43:

And the Lord said to Moses, "Say to the people of Israel, On the fifteenth day of this seventh month and for seven days is the feast of booths to the Lord. On the first day shall be a holy convocation; you shall do no laborious work. Seven days you shall present offerings by fire to the Lord; on the eighth day you shall hold a holy convocation and present an offering by fire to the Lord; it is a solemn assembly; you shall do no laborious work.

"These are the appointed feasts of the Lord, which you shall proclaim as times of holy convocation, for presenting to the Lord offerings by fire, burnt offerings and cereal offerings, sacrifices and drink offerings, each on its proper day; besides the sabbaths of the Lord, and besides your gifts, and besides all your votive offerings, and besides all your freewill offerings, which you give to the Lord.

"On the fifteenth day of the seventh month, when you have gathered in the produce of the land, you shall keep the feast of the Lord seven days; on the first day shall be a solemn rest, and on the eighth day shall be a solemn rest. And you shall take on the first day the fruit of goodly trees, branches of palm trees, and boughs of leafy trees, and willows of the brook; and you shall rejoice before the Lord your God seven days. You shall keep it as a feast to the Lord seven days in the year; it is a statute forever throughout your generations; you shall keep it in the seventh month. You shall dwell in booths for seven days; all that are native in Israel shall dwell in booths, that your generations may know that I made the people of Israel dwell in booths when I brought them out of the land of Egypt: I am the Lord your God."

Numbers 29:12–38:

"On the fifteenth day of the seventh month you shall have a holy convocation; you shall do no laborious work, and you shall keep a feast to the Lord seven days; and you shall offer a burnt offering, an offering by fire, a pleasing odor to the Lord, thirteen young bulls, two rams, fourteen male lambs a year old; they shall be without blemish; and their cereal offering of fine flour mixed with oil, three-tenths of an ephah for each of the thirteen bulls, two-tenths for each of the two rams, and a tenth for each of the fourteen lambs; also one male goat for a sin offering, besides the continual burnt offering, its cereal offering, and its drink offering.

"On the second day twelve young bulls, two rams, fourteen male lambs a year old without blemish, with the cereal offering and the drink offerings for the bulls, for the rams, and for the lambs, by number, according to the ordinance; also one male goat for a sin offering, besides the continual burnt offering and its cereal offering, and their drink offerings.

"On the third day eleven bulls, two rams, fourteen male lambs a year old without blemish, with the cereal offering and the drink offerings for the bulls, for the rams, and for the lambs, by number, according to the ordinance; also one male goat for a sin offering, besides the continual burnt offering and its cereal offering, and its drink offering.

"On the fourth day ten bulls, two rams, fourteen male lambs a year old without blemish, with the cereal offering and the drink offerings for the bulls, for the rams, and for the lambs, by number, according to the ordinance; also one male goat for a sin offering, besides the continual burnt offering, its cereal offering, and its drink offering.

"On the fifth day nine bulls, two rams, fourteen male lambs a year old without blemish, with the cereal offering and the drink offerings for the bulls, for the rams, and for the lambs, by number, according to the ordinance; also one male goat for a sin offering; besides the continual burnt offerings and its cereal offering, and its drink offering.

"On the sixth day eight bulls, two rams, fourteen male lambs a year old without blemish, with the cereal offering and the drink offerings for the bulls, for the rams, and for the lambs, by number, according to the ordinance; also one male goat for a sin offering; besides the continual burnt offering, its cereal offering, and its drink offerings.

"On the seventh day seven bulls, two rams, fourteen male lambs a year old without blemish, with the cereal offering and the drink offerings for the bulls, for the rams, and for the lambs, by number, according to the ordinance; also one male goat for a sin offering; besides the continual burnt offering, its cereal offering, and its drink offering.

"On the eighth day you shall have a solemn assembly: you shall do no laborious work, but you shall offer a burnt offering, an offering by fire, a pleasing odor to the Lord: one bull, one ram, seven male lambs a year old without blemish, and the cereal offering and the drink offerings for the bull, for the ram, and for the lambs, by number, according to the ordinance; also one male goat for a sin offering; besides the continual burnt offering and its cereal offering and its drink offering."

Deut. 16:13–15:

"You shall keep the feast of booths seven days, when you make your ingathering from your threshing floor and your wine press; you shall rejoice in your feast, you and your son and your daughter, your manservant and your maidservant, the Levite, the sojourner, the fatherless, and the widow who are within your towns. For seven days you shall keep the feast to the Lord your God at the place which the Lord will choose; because the Lord your God will bless you in all your produce and in all the work of your hands, so that you will be altogether joyful."

Let us now turn to the layout of the tractate.

I. The Appurtenances of the Festival: *Sukkah, Lulab.* 1:1–3:12

A. *The* sukkah *and its roofing.* 1:1–2:4

1:1–2   A *sukkah* taller than twenty cubits is invalid. Other points of invalidation.

3:3 A stolen or dried up willow branch is invalid.

3:4 How many myrtle branches, willow branches, and palm branches are required.

3:5–7 A stolen or dried up *etrog* [citron] is invalid. Suitable and unsuitable *etrogs*.

3:8 They bind up the *lulab* (palm branch, willow branch, and myrtle branch) with its own species.

3:9 Waving the *lulab* in the liturgy: At what point in the *Hallel* psalms.

3:10 Reciting the *Hallel* psalms.

3:11 Carrying the *lulab* in the Temple and in the provinces; carrying the *lulab* on the Sabbath; special problems relating to the foregoing.

3:12 Special problems relating to the foregoing.

II. The Rites and Offerings of the Festival. 4:1–5:8

A. *The Festival rites carried out on various days of the Festival.* 4:1–5:5

4:1 The *lulab* and willow branch are for six or seven days, the *Hallel* psalms and rejoicing (eating meat) for eight, dwelling in the *sukkah* and the water libation for seven, flute playing for five or six days. The *lulab* is for seven days: how so? The willow branch is for seven days: how so?

4:2 The *lulab* on the Sabbath: how so?

4:3–4 The willow branch rite: how so?

4:5 The *Hallel* psalms and rejoicing are for eight days: how so?

4:6–7 The water libation: how so?

5:1 The playing of the flute: how so?

5:2–5 The celebration of *bet hashshoebah*.

B. *The offerings.* 5:6–8

5:6 Sounding the *shofar* in the Temple rite. They sound no fewer than twenty-one notes in the Temple and no more than forty-eight.

5:7–8   The priestly courses and the offerings of animals on the eight days of the Festival.

The plan for the tractate could not be more straightforward. The framers have taken a special interest in the matter of dwelling in the *sukkah*—that is, a topic subjected to rather slight definition in Scripture itself and particularly relevant to the observance of the festival outside of the Temple. The tractate gives rules for the building of the *sukkah*, with special reference to the roofing which defines its valid state. Logically, the next question is the use of the *sukkah*, that is "dwelling" therein. The requirement to make use of a *lulab* and *etrog* next forms the bridge from the *sukkah* to the liturgy of the festival (**I.C** to **II**). For it is here that the *lulab* and *etrog*, first, are defined and, second, have their use specified. The rites and offerings of the festival form the final point of interest. As is Mishnah's way, the effort of unit **II** is to draw together and present as a comprehensive generalization a range of diverse rites, much as is the effort at Mishnah-tractates Zebahim and Menahot. This exercise in organization is successfully effected at **II.A**. **II.B** closes the tractate with further information relevant to the cult. The sequence of topics—(1) *sukkah*, (2) *lulab* and *etrog* + *Hallel* psalms, (3) liturgy of the Festival in general—cannot have been other than what it is, because of the integral relationship, in just this order, of *lulab-etrog-Hallel*-liturgy. It follows that the tractate is tight and logical, leaving no doubt of the highly disciplined character of the program and exegetical and redactional plan of the men who framed it.

1:1

[A]   [51c] *A sukkah which is taller than twenty cubits is invalid.*

[B]   *R. Judah declares it valid.*

[C]   *And one which is not ten handbreadths high,*

[D]   *one which does not have three walls,*

[E]   *or one, the light of which is greater than the shade of which,*

[F]   *is invalid.*

[I.A]   [The following discussion serves M. 1:1A: *A sukkah which is taller than twenty cubits is invalid. R. Judah declares it valid,* and also Y. Er. 1:1A: *The entry to an alleyway which is taller than twenty cubits must be lowered. R. Judah says, "It is not necessary to do so;* (it is valid to serve as a doorway and so symbolically to link the dwellings within into a single domain for purposes of carrying on the Sabbath)."] R. Yose stated what follows without specifying the name of an authority; R. Aha in the name of Rab: "Rabbis derive the requisite dimensions from the analogy of the doorway of the Temple building, and R. Judah, from the measurements of the doorway of the Porch (*ulam*) leading to the interior of the Temple."

[B]   If the measurement derives from the doorway of the Porch, then it should be sufficient even if it is forty cubits high.

[C]   For we have learned there: *The entrance to the Porch was forty cubits high, and its breadth was twenty cubits [M. Mid. 3:7A].*

[D]   R. Hiyya taught: "[It is valid in Judah's view] even if it is forty or fifty cubits high."

[E]   Bar Qappara taught, "[It is valid in Judah's view] even if it is a hundred cubits high."

[F]   Said R. Abin, "R. Judah is consistent with his views held elsewhere, and the same is so for rabbis.

[G]   "For we have learned there, *'And so with viaducts: they may move objects underneath them from place to place on the Sabbath,' the words of R. Judah. And sages prohibit [doing so] [M. Er. 9:4].*

[H]   "Just as, in that instance, you regard the projecting cornice as if it descends and closes off [the area beneath, so forming an area in which it is permitted to carry], so here, you regard the roof [of the *sukkah*] as if it descends and closes off [the area beneath, so forming the sheltered area of the *sukkah*].

[I]   "Accordingly, the view of R. Judah with respect to the *sukkah* is the same as his view with regard to the alleyway. The view of rabbis with regard to the *sukkah* is the same as their view with regard to the alleyway."

[J]   [Surely that cannot be the case, for] the two are not wholly parallel to one another.

[K]   There are items that are valid in a *sukkah* but invalid in the designation of an alleyway [through provision of a symbolic gate], and there are items that are valid in the designation of an alleyway but invalid in a *sukkah*.

[L]   The use of pronged poles is valid in a *sukkah* but invalid in designating an alleyway.

[M]   And so it has been taught: If one brought four poles [and stuck them in the ground] and spread roofing over them, in the case of a *sukkah* it is valid. In the case of setting up a symbolic gate for an alleyway, it is not valid. [In the latter case the poles are stuck outside of the gateway itself and hence do not serve, even with a pole placed on top of them, to form a symbolic gateway.]

[N]   With respect to the invalidity of such an arrangement in the case of the gateway to an alley,] that which you have said applies to those three handbreadths or more higher than the walls of the alleyway. But if they are not three handbreadths or higher than the walls of the alleyway, such an arrangement is valid.

[O]   [With respect to the invalidity of such an arrangement when the prongs are three handbreadths or more higher than the walls of the alleyway,] that is so when the prongs are not four hand-breadths apart; [in breadth, the alleyway is less than the stated measure]. But if it is four handbreadths in breadth, even if the prongs are somewhat higher, the arrangement is valid.

[P]   [Reverting to the argument of J–K:] [There are arrangements of] board-partitions valid in the case of a *sukkah,* but invalid in the case of designating the symbolic gate for an alleyway.

[Q]   And so it has been taught: If two of the walls are valid, [51d] and one is even an handbreadth high, [much too low,] the *sukkah* is valid. [In the case of the alleyway, by contrast, there must be three valid sides, the two sides and the top.]

[R]   R. Hiyya in the name of R. Yohanan: "Two must be four by four handbreadths, but the third may be even a single handbreadth, and such an arrangement is valid."

[S]   In the case of an alleyway, by contrast, it is valid only if it is closed in on all four sides.

[T]   [Again reverting to J–K:] If the contained area is ten cubits broad, in the case of a *sukkah* it is valid, and in the case of an alleyway it is invalid.

[U]   [As to what is valid for an alleyway and invalid for a *sukkah:*]. *If one trained a vine, gourd, or ivy over it, and then spread* sukkah-roofing on *[one of these], it is invalid [M.1:5A],* [but in an alleyway it does not invalidate the upper beam].

[V]   [In declaring such an arrangement valid in the case of an alley-way,] that which you have said applies to an area of two *seahs.* But if the enclosed area is greater than that, it then serves to define an area fenced around to serve as a garden, in which case one may carry only to the extent of four cubits.

[W]   *If the light is greater than the shade [M. Suk. 1:1E]* [created by the roofing], in the case of a *sukkah* it is invalid, and in the case of an alleyway, it is valid.

[X]   A *sukkah* that is roofed over is invalid, but an alley-entry that is roofed over remains valid.

[Y]   R. Aha in the name of R. Hoshaiah: "It is not the end of the
      matter that it be wholly roofed over. But if one merely placed a
      cornice four cubits wide, [it is deemed to serve as a partition, for
      the reason explained at G–H,] and so it permits [carrying] in the
      entire alleyway [as if it formed a partition]."

[II.A]   [What is the reason that sages declare a *sukkah* taller than twenty
         cubits to be invalid?] In the case of a house a good bit taller than
         this, is it possible that it does not require a parapet? [If the
         sukkah is analogous to a house, then if a *sukkah* is invalid at the
         specified height, do houses also fall from the category of laws
         governing dwellings at that same height?]

[B]   Is it not liable to have a *mezuzah* [on the doors]?

[C]   [The difference is this:] A house is roofed over, and a *sukkah* is
      not roofed over.

[D]   [That is not entirely so. For] we find the case of *sukkah*-roofing
      which is treated as equivalent to the roof of a house.

[E]   For we have learned there: *If the distance from the wall to the*
      sukkah-*roofing is three handbreadths, it is invalid [as a* sukkah*]*
      [M. 1:10/I].

[F]   [The difference between a *sukkah* and a house is this:] A house
      is surrounded by walls on four sides, but a *sukkah* is not sur-
      rounded by walls on four sides.

[G]   And lo, there is the case of a portico, which is open through its
      entire length to the public domain, [and yet,] R. Ila in the name
      of Rab, and R. Yohanan, both say, "They carry about [objects on
      the Sabbath] through the whole of it."

[H]   What is the upshot of the matter [to tell us why a *sukkah* taller
      than twenty cubits is invalid]?

[I]   R. Abbahu in the name of R. Yohanan: "The Torah has said,
      'You shall dwell in booths for seven days; all that are native in
      Israel shall dwell in booths' (Lev. 23:42).

[J]   "[If the roof is] up to twenty cubits, you sit in the shade of the
      sukkah. [If the roof is] more than twenty cubits high, you no
      longer are sitting in the shade of a *sukkah* but rather in the shade
      of the walls."

[K]   [As to the invalidity of a *sukkah* more than twenty cubits high,] said R. Jonah, "that which you have said applies to a case in which the *sukkah*-roofing is set higher than twenty cubits up the walls. But if it was set lower than twenty cubits up the walls, it is valid. [If the *sukkah*-roofing itself is not twenty cubits off the ground, even though the walls are higher than that, the *sukkah* is valid.]"

[L]   Said to him R. Yose, "In accord with your view, in emphasizing the location of the *sukkah*-roofing on the walls, we should repeat the Mishnah's wording as follows: 'A *sukkah* which is set more than twenty cubits up the walls is invalid.'"

[III.A]   [As to the invalidity of a *sukkah* more than twenty cubits high,] R. Ba in the name of Rab: "That applies to a *sukkah* that will hold only the head and the greater part of the body of a person and also his table.

[B]   "But if it held more than that, it is valid [even at such a height]."

[C]   [Giving a different reason and qualification,] R. Jacob bar Aha in the name of R. Josiah: "That applies [further] when the walls do not go all the way up with it [to the top, the roofing] but if the walls go all the way up with it to the roofing, it is valid."

[D]   [Proving that C's reason, not A–B's, is valid, we cite the following:]

[E]   Lo, the following Tannaitic teaching differs [in T.'s version]: **Said R. Judah, "M'SH B: The *sukkah* of Helene was twenty cubits tall, and sages went in and out, when visiting her, and not one of them said a thing."**

[F]   **They said to him, "It was because she is a woman, and a woman is not liable to keep the commandment of sitting in a *sukkah*."**

[G]   **He said to them, "Now did she not have seven sons who are disciples of sages, and all of them were dwelling in that same *sukkah*!"** [T. Suk. 1:1].

[H]   Do you then have the possibility of claiming that the *sukkah* of Helene could not hold more than the head and the greater part of the body and the table of a person? [Surely, someone of her wealth would not build so niggardly a *sukkah*.]

[I]   Consequently, the operative reason is that the sides of the *sukkah* do not go all the way up [to the *sukkah*-roofing at the top, leaving a space].

[J]   It stands to reason, then, that what R. Josiah has said is so.

[K]   [And the Tannaitic teaching] does not differ [from sages' view], for it is the way of the rich to leave a small bit of the wall out beneath the *sukkah*-roofing itself, so that cooling air may pass through.

[IV.A]   R. Hoshaiah raised the following question: "[In the case of a *sukkah* twenty cubits tall,] if one brought a plank [suitable for serving as *sukkah*-roofing] and placed it [at an angle] on the piece of a column [ten handbreadths high, set in the middle of the *sukkah*], it is obvious that if one should measure from the board [which extends at an angle upward to the roof of the *sukkah*], there is a distance of twenty cubits [or more, as the board projects beyond the *sukkah*-roofing]. If, on the other hand, one measures from the ground [to the height of the pillar, that is, the point at which the board is located], there is not a distance of twenty cubits.

[B]   "How do you treat [the *sukkah*-roofing that is above the ground but not above the board]?

[C]   "Is it deemed equivalent to invalid air space, or to invalid *sukkah*-roofing? [That is, in line with M. 1:11, *sukkah*-roofing may not be four cubits distant from the wall. The board that protrudes above twenty cubits is equivalent to a suspended side of a *sukkah*. In accord with M. 1:10, if a suspended side is three handbreadths above the ground, it is invalid. Now the problem is clear. If we take as definitive the part of the board outside of the upper ceiling of the *sukkah*, then it encompasses contained air space too large to constitute a valid *sukkah*. How much? Three handbreadths is the criterion. If we take account of the part of the board within the *sukkah* but separated from the wall, then if the *sukkah*-roofing is four handbreadths or more from the wall, it is invalid.]

[D]   "If you treat it by the criterion of invalid contained air space, it invalidates at the measure of three handbreadths.

[E]   "If you treat it by the criterion of invalid *sukkah*-roofing, it invalidates only at the measure of four cubits."

[F]   R. Yose b. R. Bun in the name of Hezekiah: "On what account did they rule, 'Invalid *sukkah*-roofing imparts invalidity only in the measure of four cubits?' It is because the *sukkah*-roofing only falls within the permissible dimensions of the *sukkah* to begin with [and a valid *sukkah* must be four by four cubits]."

[G]   [Reverting to Hoshaiah's question, A–E,] said R. Miasha, "I am amazed that R. Hoshaiah should raise such a question! Why should he not derive the answer from the statement of R. Ba bar Mamel?

[H]   "For we have learned there: *He who suspends the sides of the* sukkah *from above to below [that is, suspending the partitions from the roof], if they are three handbreadths above the ground, the* sukkah *is invalid [M. 1:10A–C].*

[I]   "In this regard R. Ba bar Mamel said, 'That applies when he does not sit and eat in the shade of the partitions. But if he was sitting and eating in the shade of the partitions, it is valid.' [Along these same lines, Hoshaiah can now answer his question. Just as Ba bar Mamel invokes the principle that we treat a partial wall as if it were complete, so we treat the pillar in the same way. If then one sits and eats in the area in which the pillar's covering diminishes the height of the *sukkah*, the area he uses as a *sukkah* is valid. Why then should Hoshaiah have asked about invalidating measurements, when, under the stated conditions, it is not an invalid situation?]"

[J]   Said R. Yose, "The statement of R. Ba bar Mamel does not teach us anything at all. R. Ba bar Mamel derived his statement from the Mishnah, for we have learned:

[K]   "*A balcony which is above water—they do not draw water from it on the Sabbath unless they made for it a partition ten handbreadths high, whether above or below [M. Er. 8:8].* [We have a balcony over the water. A hole in the floor of the balcony permits drawing water. But it is not permitted to do so on the Sabbath, because the balcony is private domain, and the water is neutral domain (*karmelit*). If a partition marks off a part of the water and makes it into private domain, however, whether this partition is located under the water or above it (K), then it is permitted to draw water on the Sabbath, that is, from private domain to private domain. Now in this case we introduce the principle invoked by Ba bar Mamel at I. We treat the partial wall as if it were complete. He derived that principle for the *sukkah* from the present one. The criticism of his position will be resumed at M.]

[L]   "In this regard, R. Zeira, R. Judah in the name of Rab: 'And that is the case only when the partition goes down into the water the measure of the dipper [so that when the dipper goes in to take up the water, it remains in demarcated, private domain].'"

[M]   [Reverting to the criticism of Ba bar Mamel's position:] But the two cases really are not parallel. The sea is an intermediate domain, *karmelit*, which is neither private nor public domain.

[N]   But here [one cannot invoke the principle of an imaginary extension of the wall], for the Torah has said, "You shall dwell in booths" (Lev. 23:42). From the very ground of the *sukkah* you measure twenty cubits. [The principle of the imaginary extension of the walls is precluded.]

[V.A.]   If a *sukkah* was lower than ten handbreadths, and one hung up in it garlands [of produce, as decorations] which are suitable to serve as *sukkah*-roofing, the garlands diminish the height of the *sukkah* to less than what is required [ten handbreadths], so that the *sukkah* is invalid.

[B]   But if not [that is, if the garlands are not suitable to serve as *sukkah*-roofing], while they diminish the height of the *sukkah*, they do not invalidate it.

[C]   If a *sukkah* was taller than twenty handbreadths, and one hung up in it garlands [as decorations] which are suitable to serve as *sukkah*-roofing, the garlands diminish the height of the *sukkah* to less than its excessive height, so that the *sukkah* is valid.

[D]   But if not, while they diminish the height of the *sukkah*, they do not validate it. [In the case of C, the garlands suitable to serve as *sukkah*-roofing are deemed to do so, with the result that, hanging down as they do, they diminish the height of the ceiling to what is within the required limits.]

[E]   Said R. Shimi, "As they have stated a rule for what is placed on top [as decoration], so they stated a rule as to what is placed on the floor.

[F]   "Straw and stubble [placed on the floor of the *sukkah*] do not serve to diminish its height; dirt and pebbles do serve to diminish the height. [The former rot and would not be used in a normal dwelling.]"

[G] Said R. Yose b. R. Bun, "If grass grew up in the *sukkah,* it does not serve to diminish the distance between the roof and the ground."

[VI.A] How do we know that air space ten handbreadths above the ground constitutes a different domain [from the ground]?

[B] R. Abbahu in the name of R. Simeon b. Laqish: "'There I will meet with you, and from above the mercy seat, from between the two cherubim that are upon the ark of the testimony, I will speak with you of all that I will give you in commandment for the people of Israel' (Ex. 25:22).

[C] "And it is written, 'Thus you shall say to the people of Israel: You have seen for yourselves that I have talked with you from heaven' (Ex. 20:22).

[D] "Just as 'speaking' stated elsewhere refers to a distinct domain [that is, heaven is distinct from earth], so 'speaking' stated here refers to a distinct domain."

[E] But was not the ark nine [and not ten] handbreadths high?

[F] A member of the household of R. Yannai said, "The mercy seat [in addition] was a handbreadth [in height]."

[G] R. Zeira asked, "How do we know that the mercy seat was a handbreadth in height?"

[H] R. Hananiah bar Samuel taught, "To all utensils that were in the Temple the Torah assigned a length, breadth, and height, except for the mercy seat, to which the Torah assigned a length and breadth, but not a height.

[I] "You may derive it from the smallest utensil in the Temple: 'And you shall make around it a frame a handbreadth wide, and a molding of gold around the frame' (Ex. 25:25). Just as here we have the height of a handbreadth, so there [with regard to the mercy seat] the height is a handbreadth."

[J] Or perhaps the meaning is, "You shall make a molding of gold around the frame," meaning, "Just as here [in the case of the molding,] the height is any measure at all, so there [in the case of the mercy seat] it may be any measure at all"!

[K]   What is the upshot of the matter?

[L]   R. Eliezer bar Jacob says, "'[And the priest shall dip his finger in the blood and sprinkle it seven times before the Lord] in front of [the veil]' (Lev. 4:17). And 'front' can only be a handbreadth."

[M]   R. Yose raised the question, "Now in the case of a tall cupboard which stands in the house, of whatever height [even above ten handbreadths], is it possible that one is not permitted to make use of what is in it, taking it out of the cupboard and using it in the house, or to put something from the rest of the house back into the cupboard?

[N]   "But [Lev. 4:17] deals with the time that the priest is [tossing the blood seven times] in the various directions. [That verse has no bearing upon our question, because it deals with the quite separate matter of tossing the blood in various directions.]"

[O]   [Reverting to the dimensions specified above, A, and, further, referring to M. Kel. 17:10: *R. Meir says, "All measurements of the Temple were according to the cubit of middle size. . . ." R. Judah says, "The standard of the cubit used for the building was six handbreadths, and for the utensils five handbreadths."*] Now the attempted proof poses no problems to the view of him who says that all measurements were in accord with the standard of six handbreadths to a cubit. [This applied throughout.]

[P]   But in accord with him who said that the measure had five handbreadths to a cubit, would the ark then not have been seven and a half handbreadths [rather than nine]? [The scriptural dimension is a cubit and a half, hence, seven and a half handbreadths, not nine.]

[Q]   R. Jacob bar Aha said, "[We deal with] a member of the house of R. Yannai and R. Simeon b. Yehosedeq. One party derives the measurement [of ten handbreadths from the ground as a domain] from the height of the ark [as above, E–F], and the other party derives the measurements from the height of a wagon. And we do not know who derived the measurement from the height of the ark and who derived it from the height of a wagon."

[R]   It stands to reason that it is the member of the house of R. Yannai who derives the measurement from that of the ark, for the members of the household of R. [52a] Yannai said, "The ark was nine handbreadths in height and the mercy seat was one handbreadth in height."

[S]   Then R. Simeon b. Yehosedeq derives the stated measurement from the wagon.

[T]   R. Zeira asked, "How do we know that the wagons [used in the Temple] were ten handbreadths high?"

[U]   Said R. Yose, "And even if you say they were ten handbreadths high, did not R. Nehemiah teach, 'The upholstered wagons were vaulted like tilted carts'? [Hence it was possible to get at the contents only through the door.]

[V]   "Now in the case of a hole in the public domain, ten handbreadths deep and four broad, is it possible to suppose that it is not forbidden to make use of what is in it in the public domain, or what is in the public domain in it? [Of course, it is prohibited to do so, since this constitutes a domain unto itself. How would the case of the wagon—a distinct high place in public domain—supply a useful analogy?]

[W]   "But when they [on the Sabbath] extended the boards from one wagon to the next, they were straight-walled [and not arch-covered]. [Accordingly, the wagons at that point were demonstrably ten handbreadths high, and, in that ordinary condition, without attention to the vault or arch, they supply a usable analogy.]"

[VII.A]   It has been taught: Rabbi says, "A *sukkah* must be four cubits by four cubits, even though it does not have four walls" [cf. T. Suk. 2 : 2F].

[B]   R. Simeon says, "It must have four walls, even though it is not four cubits square."

[C]   R. Judah says, "It must be four cubits square, or it must have four walls."

[D]   And so does R. Judah declare the *sukkah* liable to have a *mezuzah*, even though it is not four cubits by four cubits [in area] or does not have four walls.

[E]   It stands to reason that R. Judah will concur with these rabbis [A, B,] but these rabbis will not agree with R. Judah [C].

[F]   That is, even though it is four cubits by four cubits, and it has four walls, [the rabbis cited above] will still maintain that it is exempt from the requirement of having a *mezuzah* [since it is not a dwelling at all], and it also does not serve to place produce brought within it into the status of produce that has not yet been tithed but requires tithing [as bringing produce into a home imposes such status on produce brought in from the field].

[G]   R. Simeon says, "It must have four [walls]."

[H]   Rabbis say, "Three."

[I]   What is the scriptural basis for the position of the rabbis [who accept a *sukkah* in which two walls are of appropriate dimensions, and the third even a handbreadth in height, as against Simeon, who wants three of requisite dimensions, and a fourth even a handbreadth in height (cf. **VII.Y,** below)]?

[J]   The word for "living in booths" [*sukkot*] is written three times, lo, yielding three [walls], one referring to the *sukkah*-roofing above, and two referring to the walls beneath. And the requirement of yet a third wall [the little one, derives merely] from the teaching of the scribes.

[K]   What is the scriptural basis for the view of R. Simeon?

[L]   "You shall dwell in booths for seven days; all that are native in Israel shall dwell in booths, that your generations may know that I made the people of Israel dwell in booths when I brought them out of the land of Egypt: I am the Lord your God" (Lev. 23:42–43).

[M]   The word for booths [in the plural, *sukkot,*] is written once fully spelled out and twice defectively, thus four times in all, with one such reference applying to the *sukkah*-roofing above, and three to the walls below; the fourth wall derives from the requirement of the scribes [and hence of other than normal proportions].

[N]   R. Hiyya bar Ada said, "There are two Amoras. One supplied the scriptural basis for the view of rabbis, and the other, that for the view of R. Simeon.

[O]   "What is the scriptural basis for the position of the rabbis?

[P]   " 'It will be for a shade by day from the heat, and for a refuge and a shelter from the storm and rain' (Is. 4:6). Lo, this then refers to the *sukkah*-roofing above, and the three times that the *sukkah* is mentioned [at Lev. 23:42–43] supply the requirement that there be three walls.

[Q]   "What is the scriptural basis for the position of R. Simeon?

[R]   " 'It will be for a shade by day from the heat, and for a refuge and a shelter from the storm and rain' (Is. 4:6). Lo, this then refers to the *sukkah*-roofing above.

[S]   "Then [as before] the word for booths is written once fully spelled out and twice defectively, thus four times in all."

[T]   Rabbis of Caesarea derive the basis for the view of R. Simeon and the basis for the view of rabbis from the following verse: "It will be for a shade by day from the heat, and for a refuge and a shelter from the storm and rain" (Is. 4:6).

[U]   "It will be for a shade by day from the heat"—lo, one time.

[V]   "And for a refuge and a shelter"—two.

[W]   "From the storm and rain"—rabbis treat the storm and rain as a single reference.

[X]   R. Simeon treats the storm and rain as two distinct references.

[Y]   And so it has been taught: **And sages say, "[A *sukkah* is valid if] two accord with the requirement of the law, and a third, even a handbreadth in height." [R. Simeon says, "The third also must be in accord with the requirement of the law, but the fourth may be even a handbreadth in height" (T. Suk. 1:13A–B).]**

[VIII.A]   R. Hiyya in the name of R. Yohanan: "If two walls are four by four handbreadths and the third is even a handbreadth, the *sukkah* is valid."

[B]   R. Hoshaiah raised the following question: "If one placed the wall the size of a handbreadth in between, [but not in contact with, either of the valid walls,] what is the law?"

[C]   He then reverted and asked, "As to the two walls of four handbreadths which one placed in the middle [not in contact with one another], what is the law?"

[D]   R. Jacob bar Aha, "A case along these lines came to R. Yose and he declared the *sukkah* to be valid."

[E]   And so has it been taught [in T.'s version]:

[F]   **A large courtyard which is surrounded by pillars—lo, the pillars are tantamount to sides [for a *sukkah*]. (Even though the** pillars form a partition between the roof and the *sukkah*-roofing, the *sukkah* is valid) [T. Suk. 1:8A].

[G]   [with reference to C, above,] and lo, there is a Tannaitic teaching that differs: **If two were made in accord with the law [T. Suk. 1:13A],** they are valid, and if not, they are not valid. [The supposition of this objection is that placing a wall in the middle does not constitute doing it in accord with the law, as is now made explicit.]

[H]   They reasoned that the point was that we speak of a wall in the middle [as explained at F, hence Yose's ruling is contradicted].

[I]   Said R. Samuel bar R. Isaac, "[When the Tosefta speaks of not being set up in accord with the law, it means] setting up one wall not in relationship with the other valid wall [but extending one wall in one direction, another in a different direction]. [In such a case we do not have walls properly set up in accord with the law. But as to setting up a wall in the middle, there is no objection.]"

[J]   Rab said, "The wall that is only a handbreadth high has to be set out from a valid wall by a distance of a handbreadth [so that it will be visible as a separate and distinct wall]."

[K]   [Differing from this view,] Samuel said, "Even if it is right up against a valid wall, it is acceptable, for people see it as if it protrudes [as a valid wall on its own, so the *sukkah* will not appear to have only two walls, even under such conditions]."

[L]   R. Ba, Hinena bar Shelamayyah, R. Jeremiah in the name of Rab: "Even if it is right up against a valid wall, it is acceptable, for people see it as if it protrudes [as a valid wall on its own, as above]."

[M]   R. Jacob bar Aha said, "R. Yohanan and R. Simeon b. Laqish: One concurred with this party, and the other concurred with that."

[N]   Kahana and Asa came and discussed the matter before Rab, [ultimately coming out] in accord with the position of Samuel.

[O]   R. Judah bar Pazzi in the name of R. Joshua b. Levi: "And that is the case if it is set within three handbreadths [of a valid wall], as in the case of a [symbolic] gateway."

[IX.A]   R. Simeon b. Laqish said in the name of R. Judah b. Hananiah, "If one inserted four reeds into the four corners of a vineyard and tied a thread above [the reeds, from one to another], it affords protection as a braid, [that is, it forms a partition with regard to mixed seeds, and it is therefore permitted to sow seed near the vineyard, as if the vineyard were separated from the seed by a wall]. [This braided partition suffices for such a purpose.]"

[B]   [Such a construction would not serve as a gateway to link an alley-way, however, and hence, rejecting this view,] said R. Yohanan, "As is the rule governing partitions for the purposes of the Sab-bath, so is the rule defining a suitable partition in the case of mixed seeds in a vineyard."

[C]   Said R. Yohanan, "There was the case in which R. Joshua b. Qorha went to R. Yohanan b. Nuri in Nagninar. He showed him a field, which was called, 'The area close by its fellow' [because there were other seeds sown cheek by jowl with this field, sepa-rated from it by a fence]. Now in the fence there were breaches of a breadth of more than ten handbreadths. [Yohanan] would then take pieces of wood and fill up the gaps, or take reeds and fill up the gaps, so that he lessened the breaches to under ten handbreadths. He said to him, 'As is the rule for repairing this fence, so is the rule for a proper partition for the purposes of the Sabbath.'" [This illustrates Yohanan's position that a single defi-nition applies to fences for the purposes of both mixed seeds and the Sabbath.]

[D]   Said R. Zeira, "R. Simeon b. Laqish concurs with regard to the Sabbath that a braided partition does not afford protection in a gap larger than ten handbreadths. [The partition will not close off a huge gap.]"

[E]   Said R. Haggai, "The Mishnah has made the same point:

[F]   "They surround [the camp] with three ropes one above the other, on condition that between one rope and the next there be no space more than three handbreadths. The size of the ropes must be so that their [total] thickness is more than a handbreadth, so that the whole will be ten handbreadths high [M. Er. 1:9]. [If ropes are used they must be set within three handbreadths of another. If the ropes all together measure a bit more than a hand-breadth, then the entire rope fence will be ten handbreadths.]

[G]   "Now if you say that a braid affords protection for a space of more than ten handbreadths, along these same lines a single rope should do the same. [Creating the shape of a doorway serves only for ten handbreadths' breach.]"

[H]   R. Jonah said R. Hoshaiah asked about the rule pertaining to the braid: "Is it placed above or at the side?

[I]   "If you say that it may be set on top [and that serves to create the shape of a doorway], then all the more so it may be set on the side [where it surely creates a symbolic gateway].

[J]   "But if you say it may be set on the side, lo, as to setting it on top, that should not be done.

[K]   "If you say it is set on top, R. Haggai spoke well.

[L]   "If you say it is set on the side, then R. Haggai has said nothing whatsoever [at E–F]."

[M]   [Y. Suk omits:] [Why do you say so?] What is your choice? If it is placed on top, lo, it serves on top [to fill up a breach of ten handbreadths], and if it is set on the side, lo, on the side [it fills the same gap]. [Why reject Haggai's statement, E–F?]

[N]   [Interpreting Haggai's position,] Rabbis of Caesarea is the name of R. Jeremiah: "Apply the law to a case in which the reeds were in the form of poles [broad at the top and narrow at the bottom]. [The Mishnah at M. Er. 1:9 speaks of poles that are broad on top and narrow on the bottom. At the sides, then, the poles are narrow and will not hold a rope more than ten handbreadths in length. But if the rope is stretched across the top, the poles will serve for an even greater distance.]"

[O]   R. Zeira, R. Abedimi of Haifa in the name of R. Simeon b. Laqish: "As to height, even up to a hundred cubits [the thread will be suspended properly, and the partition will serve quite adequately]."

[P]   Said R. Yudan, "That which you have said applies to the matter of making a partition to prevent the appearance of mixed seeds in a vineyard, but so far as creating a partition to allow carrying on the Sabbath, braided partitions of this kind should not be higher than the roof."

[Q]   Said R. Yose, "The same rule governing a partition applies both for a partition with regard to mixed seeds in a vineyard and a partition for purpose of allowing carrying in a courtyard on the Sabbath."

[R]   In the view of R. Yose, what is the difference between setting up a beam [as a symbolic gateway] and a partition made by a braid?

[S]   A symbolic gateway constituted by a beam affords protection, [that is, constitutes suitable unification of the courtyard within, for purposes of carrying on the Sabbath] even if it is on only a single side [of the courtyard]. A braid, by contrast, affords protection only if it surrounds the courtyard on all four sides.

[T]   Now what has been said accords with the statement of R. Zeira in the name of R. Hamnuna, "A braided partition affords protection only if it forms an enclosure on all four sides."

[U]   Said R. Ba bar Mamel, "Balconies that overhang vineyards—it is forbidden to carry underneath them [on the Sabbath], for they are regarded as an extension of the roof [of the house]."

[V]   But does not the extension of the roof of a house afford protection as a braided partition?!

[W]   Said R. Phineas, "A case came before R. Jeremiah involving four columns on which were four pestles, and he permitted carrying beneath them on the Sabbath because [they afforded protection as] braided partitions."

[X]   R. Bun and [a different] R. Bun asked before R. Zeira, "As to a braid, what is the law on its serving in the case of a *sukkah*? [That is, is the shape of a gateway formed in this way serviceable as a wall for a *sukkah*?]"

[Y]   He said to them, "A braid serves in the case of a *sukkah*."

[Z]   "As to the overhanging *sukkah*-roofing, what is the law concerning it?"

[AA]   He said to them, "The overhanging *sukkah*-roofing does not serve [to form a wall] in a *sukkah*. What difference would there be between that and this?"

[BB]   [He replied,] "This [the shape of a doorway] has been made to serve as a wall [of a *sukkah*], but that [the overhanging ends of the *sukkah*-roofing] has not been made for that purpose."

[CC]   Said R. Abbahu, "All of this discussion is for the purpose of give and take. But as to instruction, it is forbidden to give a decision [that such a construction may serve as a wall for a *sukkah*]."

[DD]   Now if in the case of a *sukkah*, which is subject to a lenient rule, you maintain that view, that such a partition is forbidden [to serve as a wall], as to the Sabbath, which is subject to a stricter rule, is it not an argument *a fortiori* [that a braided wall will not serve as a suitable partition, or symbolic doorway, to permit carrying in a courtyard]?

[EE]   R. Bun bar Hiyya asked before R. Zeira, "Who taught that a braided partition *will* serve? Is it not R. Yohanan b. Nuri [= C]?"

[FF]   He said to him, "Yes, that is the case, but he is a single authority [as against the majority]."

[X.A]   [With reference to M. Kil. 4:4: *If the space between the reeds of a reed partition was less than three handbreadths, which would suffice for a kid to enter, it is deemed a valid partition. If a fence was breached for a space of ten cubits, such may be deemed an entrance. If it is wider than this, it is forbidden to sow opposite the breach. If many breaches were made in the fence, yet what is yet standing is greater than the area that is broken down, it is permitted to sow opposite the breach; if the broken down part is broader than the standing part, it is forbidden:*] You turn out to rule as follows:

[B]   As to mixed seeds in a vineyard [in which a fence must be erected to keep distinct the patches of a field sown in different seeds], if there is a breach less than three handbreadths, it is as if it were closed up.

[C]   If the breach were from three to four handbreadths, if the standing part of the fence is greater than the broken down part of the fence, it is permitted [to sow sccds by the breach, as if it were a fully valid fence], and if the breaches were greater than the standing part of the fence, it is forbidden.

[D]   If the breaches were from four to ten handbreadths, if the standing part of the fence was greater than the broken down part, it is permitted [to sow opposite the breaches]. If the broken down part is greater than the standing part, then opposite the standing part of the fence it is permitted to sow [seeds of a different sort from what is on the other side of the fence], and in the area opposite the breach, it is forbidden.

[E]   If it is greater than ten handbreadths, even though the standing part of the fence is greater than [52d] the broken down part of the fence, while it is permitted to sow opposite the standing part of the fence, it is forbidden to sow opposite the broken down part of the fence.

[F]   Now as to the matter of the Sabbath [in constructing a partition to permit carrying in a courtyard]: Any case where there is a breach less than three handbreadths, it is as if it were fully closed up.

[G]   If there is a breach from three to four handbreadths,

[H]   from four to ten, if the part of the fence that was standing is greater than the part that was breached, it is permitted [to carry in the courtyard].

[I]   If the part that was broken down was greater than the part that was standing it is forbidden [to carry].

[J]   If the breach was greater than ten handbreadths, even though the standing part of the fence was greater than the broken down part, it is forbidden [to carry in the courtyard].

[K]   Said R. Hananiah, R. Judah b. Pazzi in the name of R. Yohanan, "There is no need here [G] to refer to a gap of from three to four handbreadths."

[L]   [Why not?] One may have here a breach of three handbreadths and not have a place in which four handbreadths [of fence are actually standing].

[M]   R. Mana objected [to K], "But have we not learned, *They may surround a camp with reeds [M. Er. 1:10]?* [Now Hananiah has maintained that so small a gap as four handbreadths need not be specified at all. Yet] does a reed take up any space at all? [Yet it can be used to create a partition.]"

[N]   He said to him, "Do not answer me with reference to a breach of less than three handbreadths, for a breach less than three hand-breadths is regarded as if it were closed up."

[O]   R. Yose b. R. Bun in the name of Rab: "In any event, since the standing part of the fence is greater than the broken down part, it is permitted [to carry in that area]."

[XI.A]   The tips of lathes [used for the *sukkah*-roofing] that protrude from the *sukkah* are treated as part of the *sukkah*.

[B]   R. Hunah in the name of rabbis over there: "That is on condition that the lathes protrude across the entire face of the [*sukkah*]."

[C]   R. Jacob bar Aha, R. Yose, R. Yohanan in the name of R. Hoshaiah: "And the rule applies even in the area before a valid wall [which is deemed extended]."

[D]   R. Jacob bar Aha, R. Hiyya, R. Yohanan in the name of R. Hoshaiah: "And that is the case even not in the area before a valid wall. [That is, the protruding lathes are deemed themselves to form a valid wall, as they hang down from the roof.]"

[E]   In accord with the version of R. Yose [of what Yohanan said in Hoshaiah's name] there is no problem [in understanding the need for the ruling given above, A + C]. [The lathes have the effect of extending the wall.]

[F]   But in the version of R. Hiyya bar Ba, what sort of lenient rule have you laid down? [That is, you maintain that even if there is no wall in the area in which the lathes protrude, you deem it as if there is a *sukkah*-wall, so treating the lathes "as part of the *sukkah*." Now for what purpose does this rule serve in line with D?]

[G]   The ruling serves the case in which the sunshine is greater than the shade of the *sukkah* [and so, without taking account of the shadow of the lathes, we should deem the *sukkah* to be invalid]. [The lathes are deemed part of the *sukkah*, in that the shade they cast is included in the calculation of the effects of the *sukkah*-roofing.]

[XII.A]   *One the light of which is greater than its shade is invalid [M. 1:1E–F].*

[B]   Lo, if it is half and half, it is valid.

[C]   A *sukkah* bearing thin *sukkah*-roofing, the shade of which is greater than its light, remains valid. [Thus: "half and half is invalid."]

[D]   Here then you claim that where the light is equal to the shade, it is valid, and there [by inference] it is invalid.

[E]   Rabbis of Caesarea, R. Isaac bar Nahman in the name of R. Hoshaiah: "[The ruling of C applies to a case in which a *sukkah* was built using a tree as its *sukkah*-roofing. The tree was cut down for that purpose. The builder did not spread out the boughs

equally over the *sukkah,* hence creating the impression of a
sukkah with a thin covering.] So the case of the tree is different,
for it is usual [in such a case] for one branch to extend in one
direction, another in a different direction. [The issue of whether
the light is greater than the shade is not pertinent in this case.]"

The Talmud provides a substantial discussion for each of M.'s
topical clauses in sequence, furthermore bringing together parallel rulings in other tractates to enrich the context for discussion.
It would be difficult to point to a more satisfactory inquiry, on
the part of the Talmud, into the Mishnah's principles and problems. Unit **I** takes up the noteworthy parallel between M. 1:1A
and M. Er. 1:1A. The main point in both cases is the scriptural
basis for the dimensions specified by the law. The effort to differentiate is equally necessary. Hence the difference between one
sort of symbolic gateway and another, or between one wall built
for a given purpose, and another wall built for some other purpose, has to be specified. Unit **II** undertakes a complementary
discourse of differentiation. It is now between a *sukkah* and a
house. The two are comparable, since a person is supposed to
dwell in a *sukkah* during the Festival. Unit **III,** continuous with
the foregoing, further takes up the specified measurement and
explains it. Unit **IV** raises a rather difficult question, dealing
with the theory, already adumbrated, that we extend the line of a
wall or a roof or a cornice in such a way as to imagine that the
line comes down to the ground or protrudes upward. At unit **IV**
we seem to have a *sukkah*-roofing at an angle, extending from the
middle of a *sukkah* outwards, above the limit of twenty cubits.
I do not claim to have done full justice to the explanation of unit
IV. Unit **V** asks about lowering the *sukkah*-roofing by suspending decorations from it or raising the *sukkah*-floor by putting
straw or pebbles on it. Both produce the effect of bringing the
sukkah within the required dimensions as to its height. Unit **VI**
does not belong at all; it is primary at Y. Shab. 1:1. I assume it
was deemed to supplement M. 1:1C. Unit **VII** takes up the
matter of the required walls for the *sukkah,* M. 1:1D. Once
again the scriptural basis for the rule is indicated. Unit **VIII** carries forward this same topic, now clarifying the theoretical problems in the same matter. At unit **IX** we deal with an odd kind of
partition, a braid-partition. This discussion is primary to Y. Er.
1:9 and is inserted here because of **IX.X.** The inclusion of unit

X is inexplicable, except as it may form a continuous discourse with unit **IX**. It is primary at Y. Er. 1:8. Units **XI** and **XII** are placed where they are as discussioins of M. 1:1E. But only unit **XII** takes up the exegesis of M.'s language.

1:2 (L + V: 1:1)

[A] *A superannuated* sukkah—

[B] *the House of Shammai declare it invalid.*

[C] *And the House of Hillel declare it valid.*

[D] *And what exactly is a superannuated* sukkah?

[E] *Any which one made thirty days [or more] before the Festival [of Sukkot].*

[F] *But if one made it for the sake of the Festival,*

[G] *even at the beginning of the year,*

[H] *it is valid.*

[**I.**A] It has been taught: [From the viewpoint of the House of Hillel, one nonetheless] must do something new to the *sukkah* [to validate it, if it was built more than thirty days before the Festival].

[B] Associates said, "It must involve a handbreadth [of the *sukkah*-roofing]."

[C] R. Yose says, "It may be any measure at all."

[D] He who said, "It may be any measure at all," requires that whatever is done cover the entire face of the *sukkah*.

[**II.**A] The same dispute pertains to unleavened bread [for use for Passover].

[B] As to unleavened bread that is old, there is a dispute between the House of Shammai and the House of Hillel.

[C] Said R. Yose, "It represents the view of all parties [that old unleavened bread may not be used on Passover]. [Why not?]

[D] "Because the unleavened bread was not prepared for the sake of Passover, it is perfectly obvious that the one who made it did not take pains with it [to keep it from leavening at all]."

[III.A]   [In T.'s version:] **The *sukkah* made by shepherds, the *sukkah* made by field-workers in the summer, [or] a *sukkah* which is stolen—**

  [B]   **is invalid [T. Suk. 1:4A–B].**

  [C]   A *sukkah* made by Samaritans—if it is made in accord with the law pertaining to it, it is valid.

  [D]   If it is not made in accord with the law pertaining to it, it is invalid.

[IV.A]   He who makes a *sukkah* for himself—what blessing does he say?

  [B]   "Blessed . . . who has sanctified us by his commandments and commanded us to make a *sukkah*."

  [C]   If he made one for someone else?

  [D]   ". . . to make a *sukkah* for his Name."

  [E]   If one went into the *sukkah* to dwell therein, he says, ". . . Blessed . . . who has sanctified us by his commandments and commanded us to dwell in a *sukkah*."

  [F]   Once he has said that blessing over the *sukkah* on the first nights of the Festival, he does not have to say a blessing over it again thereafter.

  [G]   Hanin bar Ba in the name of Rab: "And as to a blessing for the season, ['. . . who has kept us in life . . . and brought us to this season']? Once it has gotten dark, what is the law as to his having to make mention of the season?"

  [H]   R. Hoshaiah said, "He has to make mention of the season."

  [I]   R. Ila said, "He has to make mention of the season."

  [J]   R. Zebidah said, "He has to make mention of the season."

  [K]   [Reformulating them,] R. Hiyya bar Ada treated these statements as traditions [that one had heard from another]:

  [L]   "R. Zeirah, R. Isaac bar Nahman in the name of R. Hoshaiah, R. Judah bar Pazzi in the name of R. Hama, father of R. Oshaiah: 'Once it has gotten dark, one has to make mention of the season.'"

Unit **I** glosses M. 1:2A–C. Unit **II** presents a dispute in a different matter but about the same principle. Unit **III** supplements
M. with T. Unit **IV** indicates the blessing to be said in connection with making and using the *sukkah*.

1:3 (L + V: 1:2)

[A]   *He who makes his* sukkah *under a tree is as if he made it in [his]
house.*

[B]   *A* sukkah *on top of a* sukkah—

[C]   *the one on top is valid.*

[D]   *And the one on the bottom is invalid.*

[E]   *R. Judah says, "If there are no residents in the top one, the
bottom one is valid."*

[I.A]   In the case of two *sukkah*-roofs, one on top of the other, in which
the upper roofing was such that the light was greater than the
shade [and hence invalid], while the lower one was such that the
light was not greater than the shade on its own, but, together
with the other roof, the shade was greater than the light—

[B]   What is the maximum of space that may be between the two
roofs so that they should be deemed joined together [into a single
sukkah-roofing, hence a valid one for the *sukkah* beneath]?

[C]   There were two Amoras. One said, "Ten cubits," and the other
said, "Four."

[D]   The one who maintained that ten cubits distance are permissible
objected to the one who said that only four are permissible, "If
it is because of the principle of forming a tent [that you want the
two so close together], we find that a tent may be no more than a
handbreadth [in its principal dimensions, hence also height]. [So
you permit too broad a space between the two roofs.]"

[II.A]   *R. Judah says, "If there are no residents in the top one, the
bottom one is valid"* [M. 1:3E].

[B]   Is the law that there must actually be residents above [to invalidate the one beneath], or may it merely be suitable for residents
[to invalidate the one beneath]?

[C]   On the basis of what a certain elder said to R. Zeira, "And even the one beneath is valid," [we may derive the answer].

[D]   For someone does not say, "Even," unless he concurs with what has been said before.

[E]   Consequently the answer is that if there actually are residents, the lower one is invalid, but if the upper one merely is suitable to serve residents, the lower one remains valid.

The point is that the roof of the *sukkah* must be exposed to the firmament and not made up, A, in large part by the boughs of the tree. D follows the same principle, now with reference to a *sukkah* covered by another. Judah's view is that, without residents, the upper *sukkah* does not constitute a dwelling, thus excluding A's consideration. Unit **I** clarifies M. 1:3B's notion of two *sukkah*-roofs near one another by raising a problem independent of M. Unit **II** amplifies Judah's meaning, M. 1:3E.

1:4 (L + V: 1:3)

[A]   *[If] one spread a sheet on top of [a* sukkah*] on account of the hot sun,*

[B]   *or underneath [the cover of boughs] on account of droppings [of the branches or leaves of the bough-cover],*

[C]   *or [if] he spread [a sheet] over a four-poster bed [in a* sukkah*],*

[D]   *it is invalid [for dwelling or sleeping and so for fulfilling one's obligation to dwell in the* sukkah*].*

[E]   *But he spreads it over the frame of a two-poster bed.*

[I.A]   It has been taught: If one suspends rugs in the *sukkah*, it remains valid.

[B]   Said R. Haninah, "That which you have said applies to suspending them on the sides of the *sukkah*. But if one suspends them at the top, it is invalid."

[II.A]   *Or underneath the cover of boughs, on account of droppings of the branches of leaves of the bough-cover [M. 1:4B]:*

[B]   Said R. Yose, "They have stated only, 'On account of droppings.' Lo, if one does so not on account of droppings, it is valid."

[III.A]   *But he spreads it over the frame of a two-poster bed [M. 1:4E].*

[B]   R. Bibi in the name of R. Yohanan: "[This cover forms a kind of covered space, of which we do not take account,] just as one may have created an enclosed space by raising his two hands [within a covering]. [Doing so has no bearing on the validity of the *sukkah;* this does not constitute a roof within the roof.]"

If, C, a four-poster bed, located in the *sukkah,* is covered over, it is not suitable as a place for sleeping in the *sukkah,* deemed to be like a *sukkah* in a house. But a two-poster bed, E, covered over has a sloping roof, which does not enter the category of a roof annulling the effects of the *sukkah*-roofing. All the three of the Talmud's units clarify M.'s rulings, as indicated.

1:5 (L + V: 1:4–5)

[A]   *[If] one trained a vine, gourd, or ivy over it and then spread sukkah-roofing on [one of these], it is invalid.*

[B]   *But if the sukkah-roofing exceeded them,*

[C]   *or if he cut them [the vines] down,*

[D]   *it is valid.*

[E]   *This is the general rule:*

[F]   *Whatever is susceptible to uncleanness and does not grow from the ground—they do not make a sukkah-roofing with it.*

[G]   *And whatever is not susceptible to uncleanness, but does grow from the ground [and has been cut off]—they do make a sukkah-roofing with it.*

[I.A]   [As to M. 1:5C,] R. Ba in the name of Rab: "[The trained vines are valid roofing when cut down, if to begin with] the man trained them for that purpose."

[B]   R. Jacob bar Aha in the name of R. Zeira: "He has to shift them about [after cutting them down, so as to indicate that they now are meant to serve the purpose of covering the *sukkah*]."

[C]   Said R. Yose, "Both rulings are intended to be lenient. Thus:

[D]   "If one trained them for this purpose [serving as *sukkah*-covering] even though he did not shift them about,

[E]   "or if he shifted them about even though he did not to begin with training them for this purpose, [the *sukkah* is valid]."

[II.A]   [Illustrating M. 1:5F–G:] R. Ba, Hinena bar Shelamayya, R. Jeremiah in the name of Rab: "If one covered a *sukkah* with wedges, it is invalid.

[B]   "If he did so with plain arrow shafts, it is valid. If he did so with bored shafts [which serve as a receptacle] it is invalid."

[C]   **[If] one made a *sukkah*-roofing of stalks of flax, it is valid.**

[D]   **[If one made a *sukkah*-roofing of] processed stalks of flax, it is invalid [T. Suk. 1:5]. [Y. reverses C and D.]**

[E]   **If one made a *sukkah*-roofing of ropes or with sheaves of grain, it is valid [T. Suk. 1:4C].**

[F]   There is a Tanna who says that [a roofing of ropes] is valid, and there is a Tanna who says that it is invalid.

[G]   He who says that such a roofing is valid speaks of roping made of bast.

[H]   He who says that such a roofing is invalid speaks of roping made of flax.

[III.A]   Said R. Yohanan: "It is written, 'You shall keep the feast of booths seven days, when you make your ingathering from your threshing floor and your wine press' (Deut. 16:13).

[B]   "From the refuse of your threshing floor and your wine press you may make *sukkah*-roofing for yourself."

[C]   R. Simeon b. Laqish said, "'But a mist went up from the earth and watered the whole face of the ground' (Gen. 2:6). [The analogy of the covering of the *sukkah* is to mist, which arises from the ground and is not susceptible to receive uncleanness.]"

[D]   Said R. Tanhuma, "This one is consistent with opinions held elsewhere, and that one is consistent with opinions held elsewhere.

[E]   "R. Yohanan has said, 'The clouds came from above,' and so he derives the rule from the reference to 'your ingathering.'

[F]   "R. Simeon b. Laqish said, 'Clouds come from below,' so he derives the rule from clouds [of mist]."

[G]   Said R. Abin, "This party is consistent with opinions held elsewhere, and that one is consistent with opinions held elsewhere.

[H]   "R. Yohanan compares the matter to one who sends his fellow a jug of wine, giving him the jug as well as the wine. [Along these same lines God gives the clouds along with the rain from heaven.]

[I]   "R. Simeon b. Laqish compares the matter to a priest, who said to his fellow, 'Send over your basket and take some grain for yourself.' [Clouds come from below, and God puts rain in them in heaven.]"

Unit **I** complements the rule of M. 1:5A–D. Units **II** and **III** take up M. 1:5F–G, what may be used in *sukkah*-roofing. Unit **II** provides some facts, and unit **III**, exegetical foundations for M.'s principle.

1:6

[A]   *Bundles of straw, wood, or brush—*

[B]   *they do not make a* sukkah-*roofing with them.*

[C]   *But any of them which one untied is valid.*

[D]   *And all of them are valid [as is] for use for the sides [of the* sukkah*].*

[I.A]   [As to M. 1:6A–B,] R. Hiyya in the name of R. Yohanan: "It is because [the *sukkah*] will look like a storage-house."

[B]   R. Jacob bar Ahayye, R. Sheshet in the name of R. Hiyya the Elder: "A bundle is made up of no fewer than twenty-five sticks [of wood]. [Fewer than these do not, when tied together, add up to a bundle.]"

[II.A]   Hinena bar Shelemayya in the name of Rab: "If one cut sheaves for use for *sukkah*-roofing, they are not regarded as having 'handles.' [That is, what is attached to them does not serve to transmit uncleanness affecting that attachment to the food contained in the sheaves themselves. In the present instance, then, if a source of uncleanness touched the straw, food in the sheaf is unaffected.]"

[B]   If one cut the sheaves to begin with for the purpose of *sukkah*-roofing and then gave thought to them for use for food, the revised intention [for the sheaves] takes effect [so that now, if an attachment of a sheaf is in contact with a source of uncleanness, food in the sheaf is made unclean, that is, the rule of "handles" comes into play].

[C]   If one cut the sheaves to begin with for food, and then gave thought to them for use for *sukkah*-roofing,

[D]   others say, "[The 'handles' take effect and transmit uncleanness in contact with them to food in the sheaf] unless the straw is larger in volume than the food in the sheaf and also than the handle [or protrusion]. [If the refuse of the sheaf is more abundant than either the food or the protrusion, the refuse annuls them, and the whole may then be used for *sukkah*-roofing.]

[E]   Rab accords with this statement by the others [at D].

[F]   How shall we treat the following case: One cut a sheaf for use for *sukkah*-roofing, and the sheaf was [wet down and so] rendered susceptible to uncleanness [but, being used for *sukkah*-roofing, is not at that point susceptible to uncleanness], and if then the farmer said, "After they have served their purpose in carrying out the religious duty [of covering the *sukkah*], I shall bring the sheaves back to the threshing floor,"

[G]   do the sheaves require being rendered susceptible to uncleanness a second time [in order to become susceptible to uncleanness],

[H]   or does the first occasion on which they were rendered susceptible suffice [since, at that point, there was no intention of using the food in the sheaves at all]? [This question is not answered.]

[III.A]   R. Yose in the name of R. Hama bar Haninah: "'[And you shall put in it the ark of the testimony,] and you shall screen the ark with the veil' (Ex. 40:3).

[B]   "On the basis of the use of the root for *sukkah*, as 'screen,' we learn that the side [of the *sukkah* also] is called *sukkah*-covering.

[C]   "On the basis of this verse, further, we learn that they may make the sides of the *sukkah* with something that is susceptible to uncleanness [since the veil is susceptible in that way]."

Used when bound up, the bundles look not like roofing but like a storage-area. The bundles in any case may serve as sides or sideposts. Unit **I** supplies a rule for M. Unit **II** points out that used for one purpose, a sheaf will not be susceptible to uncleanness, and, planned for use for another, it will be. Accordingly, we invoke the principle that protrusions of pieces of food affect the food to which they are attached when the sheaf is planned for use as food, but not when the sheaf is used for another purpose. This is relevant, in a general way, to M. 1:6A. Unit **III** provides a scriptural basis for M. 1:6D.

1:7

[A]   *"They make sukkah-roofing with boards," the words of R. Judah.*

[B]   *And R. Meir prohibits doing so.*

[C]   *[If] one put on top of it a board which is four handbreadths broad, it is valid,*

[D]   *so long as one not sleep underneath [that particular board].*

[I.A]   R. Jeremiah in the name of Rab: "The dispute applies when the board is four handbreadths broad."

[B]   R. Yose in the name of R. Yohanan: "The dispute applies to boards that have been planed for use in making utensils."

[C]   Now on the basis of what R. Jeremiah said in the name of Rab, "There is a dispute when the board is four handbreadths broad," it must follow that all parties agree that if the boards are planed for use in making utensils, it is permitted to use such boards in the roofing of a *sukkah*.

[D]   On the basis of what [52c] R. Jeremiah has said, "If one covered a *sukkah* with wedges, it is invalid,"

[E]   in connection with which they said [that Rab] decided in accord with the position of R. Meir,

[F]   it follows that [from Meir's position] the same rule applies to this
       case and to that [namely, to planks four handbreadths broad and
       to planks that have been planed].

[G]   Now as to R. Yose: in regard to what R. Yose said in the name of
       R. Yohanan, "The dispute pertains to planks that were planed
       for use in making utensils," lo, [the rule] for those four hand-
       breadths wide is that all parties concur it is forbidden to do so.

[H]   [That indeed is so, for] on the basis of R. Yose's instructions in
       the great assembly, "They may make *sukkah*-roofing out of the
       main beam of the ceiling," and they say that he gave instruction
       in accord with the view of R. Judah,

[I]   it must follow that [from the viewpoint of Judah] the same rule
       applies both in this case and in that [both boards four hand-
       breadths broad and boards that have been planed may be used
       for *sukkah* roofing].

[II.A] [As to M. 1:7C–D, that it is not permitted to sleep under a
       board of that size,] Samuel said, "That which you have said ap-
       plies to a board of the specified length. But as to one of that
       breadth, it is permitted [to sleep under it]. [If the board is set
       lengthwise through the *sukkah*, then for its entire length there
       is no valid *sukkah*-roofing at all. But if it was set breadthwise,
       one may sleep under it, for there is valid roofing on both sides
       of the board.]"

[B]   R. Yohanan and R. Simeon b. Laqish both say, "Whether it is
       set lengthwise or breadthwise, it is valid."

[C]   R. Zeriqan in the name of R. Hamnuna rules in accord with the
       view of him who declares sleeping under such a board to be
       invalid whether it is set lengthwise or breadthwise.

[D]   Rabin and R. Bun raised the question before R. Zeirah: "How is
       it possible to interpret what both R. Yohanan and R. Simeon b.
       Laqish have said [that one may sleep under such a board, since
       M. 1:7D says one may not do so]?"

[E]   He said, "It is because invalid *sukkah*-roofing invalidates only
       four cubits [whether it is located in the middle of the roof or on
       sides]. [Now when M. 1:7D says one may not sleep under such
       a board, it is in accord with the principle that invalid *sukkah*-
       roofing invalidates an area of four handbreadths. The *sukkah* it-

self remains valid, if it is a large one. But as to the view of the authority behind M. 1:7D, a *sukkah* of four cubits is deemed valid, accordingly, in his view the area beneath the board, on its own, constitutes an invalid *sukkah*.]"

[F]   The following Tannaitic teaching differs from the view of R. Hamnuna [who maintains that one may not sleep under such a board]: "In the case of a *sukkah* which has room for only one's head, the greater part of his body, and his table, one may bring a board and join three handbreadths of it [to the *sukkah*, to enlarge the *sukkah*]."

[G]   Now if you say that one does so breadthwise—one cannot say so, for R. Zeriqan ruled in the name of R. Hamnuna in accord with the view of him who declares sleeping under such a board to be invalid whether it is set lengthwise or breadthwise.

[H]   But thus we must interpret the matter: The board is set lengthwise [contrary to the view of Hamnuna, that is, permissible], and as to the authority of the cited passage it is possible that he holds one may not sleep under that board [and hence the cited passage and the rule of M. 1:7D are coherent with one another].

Boards are analogous to normal roofing material for a house. A single board may be used, but with the stated functional restriction. Unit **I** clarifies what is at issue at M. 1:7A–B. Unit **II** then explores the restriction expressed at M. 1:7C–D.

1:8 (L + V: 1:7)

[A]   *A timber roofing which had no plastering—*

[B]   *R. Judah says, "The House of Shammai say, 'One loosens it and removes one [board] between each two.'*

[C]   *"And the House of Hillel say, 'One either loosens it or removes one [board] from between each two.'"*

[D]   *R. Meir says, "One removes one from between each two, and does not loosen [the others at all]."*

[I.A]   [In the view of R. Meir], if one has loosened a board, he does not have to remove one out of every two.

The Talmud clarifies M. 1:8D.

1:9 (L + V: 1:8)

[A]   *He who makes a roof for his* sukkah *out of spits or with the side pieces of a bed—*

[B]   *if there is a space between them equivalent to their own breadth,*

[C]   *[the* sukkah*] is valid.*

[D]   *He who hollowed out a space in a haystack to make a* sukkah *therein—*

[E]   *it is no* sukkah.

[I.A]   It was taught: [The space between them (M. 1:9B)] must be greater than their own breadth.

[B]   Associates say, "[the reason for A is] that one handbreadth does not enter another handbreadth['s area]. [That is, one cannot be precise about the matter, and hence we demand a slight bit more space between them. For one cannot fit exactly something of a handbreadth into precisely that amount of open space.]"

[C]   R. Ba bar Mamel objected, "Lo, in the case of a glass utensil, it is assumed that one can insert what is a handbreadth in its measurement into the space of a handbreadth."

[D]   Said R. Yose, "In such a case, what is exactly a handbreadth may fit into the space of an exact handbreadth and also come out, while in the present case, it may fit in but then will not emerge [leaving precisely the same space]."

[II.A]   [As to M. 1:9D–E,] R. Abbahu in the name of R. Yohanan: "The reason is that it appears like a storage-bin."

[B]   R. Hiyya taught, "When Scripture says, '. . . you will make for yourself . . .' (Deut. 16:13), it means to exclude what is already made [not for the purpose of a *sukkah*, e.g., a hole in a haystack]."

[C]   What is the practical difference between these two views?

[D]   A case in which a space already has been hollowed out is at issue between them, [in a case in which, for the *sukkah*, the man hollows out a bit more].

[E]   In the the view of R. Hiyya it is valid (L + V: invalid) [because of the additional labor].

[F]   In the view of R. Yohanan it is invalid. (L + V: valid)

Unit **I** qualifies the rule of M. 1:9B. The point is minor. Unit **II** provides reasons for the rule of M. 1:9D–E.

1:10 (L + V: 1:9)

[A]   *He who suspends the sides from above to below—*

[B]   *if they are three [or more] handbreadths above the ground,*

[C]   *[the sukkah] is invalid.*

[D]   *[If he builds the sides] from the ground upward,*

[E]   *if [they are] ten handbreadths above the ground,*

[F]   *[the sukkah] is valid.*

[G]   R. Yose says, "Just as [the required height] from below to above [when the wall is built up from the ground] is ten handbreadths,

[H]   *"so [the required height] from above to below [when the wall is suspended from above toward the ground] is ten handbredths [even though the bottom is not within three handbreadths of the ground]."*

[I]   *[If] one sets the sukkah-roofing three handbreadths from the walls [of the sukkah], [the sukkah] is invalid.*

[I.A]   Said R. Yohanan, "R. Yose spoke only in regard to the matter of the *sukkah* [at M. 1:10G–H]. But as to the matter of [a partition to permit carrying in a courtyard] on the Sabbath, also R. Yose concurs [that a partition suspended more than three handbreadths above the ground is invalid]."

[B]   A statement of R. Hanina indicates that even for the matter of a partition constructed for purposes of carrying on the Sabbath, R. Yose maintains the same view [that the partition, if of requisite dimensions, is imagined to descend].

[C]   For R. Hanina said, "On the Sabbath a ruler came to Sepphoris, and they suspended rugs [in his honor, so connecting columns of a colonnade]. R. Ishmael b. R. Yose permitted carrying [in the colonnade, regarding these as adequate partitions to set off the area into a single domain], in accord with the theory of his father [Yose]."

[D]   R. Yose b. R. Bun in the name of R. Samuel bar R. Isaac, "What R. Yose b. Haninah said accords with the view of R. Hananiah, and both of them differ from R. Yohanan.

[E]   "For R. Yohanan said, R. Judah, R. Yose, and R. Hananiah b. Aqabia—all three said one thing. R. Judah's rule concerning aqueducts [that one may carry under them]; R. Yose's rule given here [**I.C**]; and R. Hananiah b. Aqabia.

[F]   "For it was taught: R. Hananiah gave a permissive ruling in three matters: He permitted [placing produce in] a large reed [kept in water, without regarding produce placed therein as having been wet down and so rendered susceptible to uncleanness]; he permitted [drawing water from] a balcony [situated over water, so regarding the sides of the balcony as descending, in imagination, into the water and so forming a single domain]; and he permitted carrying towels [to the bathhouse on the Sabbath, without scruple that someone may wring out the towel, which is not permitted]."

The point of **I.D** is that all of the three cited authorities concur that an imaginary wall is drawn downward from above and suffices for purposes of closing off the area beneath. That is the conception of Hanina in Yose's name for the Sabbath. It is the conception of Judah's rule that the two open sides of the aqueduct are deemed to descend in an imaginary wall, so closing off the area and permitting carrying underneath it. Hananiah has the same position on the balcony, with its walls descending to the water beneath. To this discussion the present rule is decidedly tangential.

1:11 (L + V: 1:10)

[A]   *A house, [the roof of] which was damaged, and on [the gaps in the roof of which] one put* sukkah-*roofing—*

[B]   *if the distance from the wall to the* sukkah-*roofing is four cubits, it is invalid [as a* sukkah].

[C]   *And so too, [is the rule for] a courtyard which is surrounded by a peristyle.*

[D]   *A large sukkah, [the roof of which] they surrounded with some sort of material with which they do not make sukkah-roofing—*

[E]   *if there was a space of four cubits below it,*

[F]   *it is invalid [as a sukkah].*

[I.A]   R. Hiyya taught, "If there is uncovered, hence invalid air space, it invalidates at a measure of three handbreadths. If there is invalid *sukkah*-roofing [as in the unroofed gap at M. 1:11B], it invalidates only at a measure of four cubits."

[B]   Said R. Yose, "We also have learned both of these rules [in the Mishnah]:

[C]   "If there is uncovered, hence invalid air space, it invalidates at a measure of three handbreadths, for we have learned: *If one sets the sukkah-roofing three handbreadths from the walls of the sukkah, the sukkah is invalid [M. 1:10/I].*

[D]   "If there is invalid *sukkah*-roofing, it invalidates only at a measure of four cubits, for we have learned: *A house, the roof of which was damaged, and on the gaps in the roof of which one put sukkah-roofing, if the distance from the wall to the sukkah-roofing is four cubits, it is invalid as a sukkah [M. 1:11A–B].*

[E]   "Lo, if the distance is less, it is valid."

[II.A]   What is the rule as to sleeping underneath it? [That is, if the owner of the *sukkah* slept under inadequately roofed-over space, hence the open air space, does he thereby carry out his obligation to dwell in the *sukkah?*]

[B]   R. Isaac b. Elishaya objected [that it is surely forbidden to sleep under that air space, for], "Lo, [the rule is that] soft mud completes [the requisite volume of natural water in an] immersion pool, yet it is forbidden to immerse in the soft mud. [One must immerse only in the water of the pool.] Here too while the area is valid as a *sukkah*, it is not valid for sleeping, [that is, for use in the way in which the *sukkah* is supposed to be used]."

[III.A]   [Reverting to I.B–E, Yose's claim that Hiyya's rules may be derived from the present Mishnah's laws, we shall now object that the parallel is not germane. There is a special reason that, in the case of a gap of *sukkah*-roofing between the wall and the roof of four cubits, the roofing is invalid.] Hezekiah said, "It is because it appears like a crooked wall. [Then invalid roofing invalidates at a measure of four cubits even in the case of a large *sukkah*, as at M. 1:11D–F.]"

[B]   R. Hoshaiah taught, "It is because it appears like a crooked wall."

[C]   R. Ba, R. Hiyya in the name of R. Yohanan: "It is because it appears like a crooked wall."

[D]   R. Zeirah, R. Yose in the name of Kahana: "It is because it appears like a crooked wall."

[E]   [In regard to all of these formulations,] said R. Jonah to R. Yose, "And why do we not say, 'It is because invalid *sukkah*-roofing invalidates only at a measure of four cubits'?"

A–B restate the point of M. 1:10I, but with a different measurement in the case in which there is roofing, not empty space, in the gap. At M. 1:11C we have a roof extending more than four cubits from the walls on the sides of the courtyard, and open space in the center. If the center is provided with *sukkah*-roofing up to within four cubits of the existing roof, it is valid. If, M. 1:11D–F, between the wall of the *sukkah* and the valid roofing, there are four cubits of invalid roofing, it is invalid. Unit **I** draws upon the Mishnah-passage before us to support Hiyya's statement, **I.A**. Unit **II** clarifies the status of an invalid part of the roofing of an otherwise valid *sukkah*. Unit **III** reverts to the proposition of unit **I**, drawing upon M. 1:11D–F.

1:12 (L + V: 1:11)

[A]   *He who makes his* sukkah *in the shape of a cone or who leaned it up against a wall—*

[B]   *R. Eliezer declares it invalid,*

[C]   *because it has no roof.*

[D]   *And sages declare it valid.*

[E]   *A large reed-mat,*

[F]   *[if] one made it for lying on, is susceptible to uncleanness, and [so] they do not make* sukkah-*roofing out of it.*

[G]   *[If one made it] for* sukkah-*roofing, they make* sukkah-*roofing out of it, and it is not susceptible to uncleanness.*

[H]   *R. Eliezer says, "All the same are a small one and a large one:*

[I]   *"[if] one made it for lying on, it is susceptible to uncleanness, and they do not make* sukkah-*roofing out of it.*

[J]   *"[If one made if for]* sukkah-*roofing, they do make* sukkah-*roofing out of it, and it is not susceptible to uncleanness."*

[I.A]   **R. Eliezer concedes [in regard to M. 1:12A–C] that if its roof is a handbreadth in size,**

[B]   **or if it was a handbreadth above the ground,**

[C]   **it is valid [T. Suk. 1:10B–D].**

[D]   It has been taught: He who makes his *sukkah* like a house in the forest of Lebanon [so that the tree trunks serve as the walls, and the *sukkah*-roofing is spread above]—it is valid.

[E]   For whom is such a ruling required?

[F]   Is it not required to clarify the position of R. Eliezer? [To him the issue is whether or not there is a clearly discernible roof, M. 1:12C, not whether the walls have been erected for the purpose of the *sukkah*.]

[II.A] Abba bar Hana in the name of R. Yohanan: "The teaching [at M. 1:12E–G] concerns mats made in Usha."

[B]   R. Eliezer said, "Mats made in Usha without specification as to their purpose are susceptible to uncleanness [for they are routinely used for lying on], unless one actually uses them for tents [for *sukkah*-roofing]. [Then their secondary use is clear.]

[C]   "Mats made in Tiberias without specification as to their use are insusceptible to uncleanness [for they are routinely used for roofing] unless one actually uses them for lying on."

[D]   R. Isaac bar Haqolah, R. Simeon b. Rabbi gave a decision in regard to mats placed over the door of stalls that they are insusceptible to uncleanness [since they are not used for lying on].

[E]   R. Imi taught: "As to a mat made of twigs for covering a *sukkah,*
       that became unclean—what is the law as to using it for *sukkah*-
       roofing?"

[F]   This is covered by the dispute between R. Eliezer and sages [at
       M. 1:12E–J].

[G]   R. Isaac bar Eleazar gave a decision that, out of necessity, it
       is permitted to make use of the end-knots of a reed-mat for
       sukkah-roofing.

[H]   We have learned: *So too if the end-knots of a reed-mat are un-
       tied, it is insusceptible to uncleanness [M. Kel. 20:7],* and you
       say this! [That is, it is not merely out of necessity, when there is
       no alternative. These knots in fact are insusceptible and there-
       fore may be used.]

       Unit **I** cites T. to clarify Eliezer's position at M. 1:12B–C. Unit
       II amplifies M. 1:12E–J, with special reference to the status of
       mats generally used for one purpose as against those generally
       used for another.

2:1

[A] [52d] *He who sleeps under a bed in a* sukkah *has not fulfilled his obligation.*

[B] *Said R. Judah, "We had the practice of sleeping under the bed before the elders, and they said nothing at all to us."*

[C] *Said R. Simeon, "M^cSH B: Tabi, Rabban Gamaliel's slave, slept under the bed.*

[D] *"And Rabban Gamaliel said to the elders, 'Do you see Tabi, my slave—he is a disciple of a sage, so he knows that slaves are exempt from keeping the commandment of dwelling in the* sukkah. *That is why he is sleeping under the bed.'*

[E] *"Thus we learned that he who sleeps under bed has not fulfilled his obligation."*

[I.A] There we have learned: *But he spreads it over the frame of a two-poster bed [M. 1:4E],*

[B] and here does the law say this [M. 2:1A]!

[C] Said R. Eliezer, "There [where it is permitted to sleep as described] he and his cloak are under the *sukkah*-roofing. But here [at M. 2:1A] he and his cloak are under the bed [under the *sukkah*-roofing]."

[II.A] The theories attributed to R. Judah are contradictory. There he has said that a concrete practice of the law takes precedence over a matter of study [at Y. Pes. 3:7], and here he has said this [that when they came to study, they would sleep under the bed, and the elders did not object]! [The supposition is that Judah claims the elders kept silent because they regarded the study as more important and were not interested in whether or not the disciples carried out their religious duties in the proper way.]

[B]   [No, there is no contradiction, and indeed the cited case is irrelevant, for] R. Judah holds the view that he who sleeps under a bed is as if he slept under the *sukkah*-roofing itself. [Hence the claimed implication is null.]

[C]   All the more so, then, are the theories attributed to R. Judah contradictory. For there we have learned: *R. Judah says, "If there are no residents in the top one, the bottom one is valid"* [M. 1 : 3E].

[D]   Lo, if there are residents in the upper *sukkah*, the lower *sukkah* is invalid. [Yet here he does not take account of the interposition of the bed between the *sukkah*-roofing and the man, while there he does take account of the interposition of the intervening floor, should there be residents thereon, between the *sukkah*-roofing and the people in the lower part of the *sukkah*.]

[E]   Said R. Yose, "There an intervening contained air space is present, while here there is no intervening contained air space."

[III.A]   The theories assigned to Rabban Gamaliel are contradictory. For it has been taught: Tabi, the slave of Rabban Gamaliel, would wear *tefillin*, and sages did not object to his doing so.

[B]   Here, by contrast, they objected to his doing so [accounting for Gamaliel's need, M. 2 : 1D, to explain himself].

[C]   He did so so as not to make the sages in the *sukkah* squeeze together [but to provide them with more space]. [Hence he made the slave sleep under the bed.]

[D]   If the operative consideration was so as not to make the sages in the *sukkah* sit cramped together, then the slave should have sat outside of the *sukkah* altogether.

[E]   Tabi, Gamaliel's slave, wanted to hear what the sages were saying [so he stayed under the *sukkah*, hence under the bed].

A's theory, in line with M. 1 : 4C–D, is that the bed constitutes a tent within the *sukkah*. One has thus not slept in the *sukkah*—under its roofing—but under the tent constituted by the bed.

The Talmud remains close to the Mishnah, providing harmoniza-
tions at all three units between what is before us and theoreti-
cally contradictory sayings or stories. Unit **I** constrasts M. 1:4E
to M. 2:1A and shows they are congruent with one another.
Units **II** and **III** compare materials on Judah and Gamaliel, re-
spectively, in other passages and again harmonize them.

2:2

[A]   *He who props his* sukkah *up with the legs of a bed—it is valid.*

[B]   *R. Judah says, "If it cannot stand on its own, it is invalid."*

[I.A] ["The reason for Judah's view,"] said R. Imi, "is that there is not
a distance of ten handbreadths between the bed and the *sukkah*-
roofing. [The *sukkah*-roofing rests on the ends of the bed. The
roofing cannot stand on its own.]"

[B]   Said R. Ba, "The reason is that they do not set up a *sukkah* on
something that is susceptible to uncleanness."

[C]   But lo, it has been taught [in T.'s version]: **MᶜSH B: The Jeru-
salemites would let down their beds through the windows
ten handbreadths high and covered over them with a *sukkah*-
roofing and slept under them [cf. M. Suk. 2:1B] [T. Suk.
2:3A].**

[D]   Now if you maintain that Judah's reason is that they do not set
up a *sukkah* on something that is susceptible to uncleanness—lo,
here is a case in which they set it on something susceptible to
uncleanness!

[E]   It must follow that the reason is only that there is not a distance
of ten handbreadths between the bed and the *sukkah*-roofing.

The Talmud supplies an account of the reason of Judah at M.

2:3

[A]   *A sukkah [the roofing of which] is loosely put together,*

[B]   *but the shade of which is greater than the light,*

[C]   *is valid.*

[D]   *The [sukkah] [the roofing of which] is tightly knit like that of a house,*

[E]   *even though the stars cannot be seen from inside it,*

[F]   *is valid.*

[I.A]   Rab and Samuel: One said that the word for "loosely put together" is "thin" (DLL), and the other that it is "loosely put together" (DBLL).

[B]   He who utilizes the word, "thin," approves such a roofing when the shade of the *sukkah*-roofing is greater than the light.

[C]   He who utilizes the word, "loosely put together," approves such a roofing [even] when the shade of the *sukkah*-roofing is not greater than the light [it lets through].

[II.A] [With reference to M. 2:3E,] is that to say that [to begin with] the stars must be visible through the *sukkah*-roofing?

[B]   R. Levi in the name of R. Hama bar Haninah: "That teaching pertains to the possibility of seeing sunshafts through the *sukkah*-roofing [and not stars by night]."

Unit **I** provides text-criticism for the word-choice at M. 2:3A, and unit **II**, an exegesis of M. 2:3E.

2:4

[A]   *He who makes his sukkah on the top of a wagon or a boat—it is valid.*

[B]   *And they go up into it on the festival day.*

[C]   *[If he made it] at the top of a tree or on a camel, it is valid.*

[D]   *But they do not go up into it on the festival day.*

[E]   *[If] two [sides of a sukkah] are [formed by] a tree, and one is made by man,*

[F]   *or two are made by man and one is [formed by] a tree,*

[G]   *it is valid.*

[H]   *But they do not go up into it on the festival day.*

[I]   *[If] three are made by man and one is [formed by] a tree, it is valid.*

[J]   *And they do go up into it on the festival day.*

[K]   *This is the governing principle: In the case of any [sukkah] in which the tree may be removed, and [the sukkah] can [still] stand by itself, it is valid.*

[L]   *And they go up into it on the festival day.*

[I.A] [With reference to M. 2:4, making a *sukkah* on a boat,] how shall we interpret the matter?

[B]   If the boat is beached, then all parties concur that it is permitted to do so.

[C]   If the boat is en route, there is a dispute between R. Eleazar b. Azariah and R. Aqiba [**II.G**].

[D]   But thus must we interpret the issue: we deal with a boat that lies in port.

[II.A] R. Simeon b. Karsena in the name of R. Aha: "R. Meir, R. Yose, and R. Eleazar all expressed the same principle."

[B]   R. Meir in connection with the sideposts [of an alleyway], for we have learned there:

[C]   *An animate creature which is used to cover up the entrance of a tomb imparts uncleanness as a sealing-stone. But R. Meir declares it clean when used for that purpose [M. Er. 1:7D–E].* [Since the beast is not set permanently at that spot, it is insusceptible to uncleanness.]

[D]   R. Yose in the matter of spreading uncleanness through overshadowing.

[E]   *For R. Yose says, "A cabin located on a boat does not have the power of spreading uncleanness to what lies in its shadow when it overshadows a corpse [M. Oh. 8:5]. [Since the boat is not affixed in one place, it does not have the effect of spreading uncleanness as does a Tent.]"*

[F]   R. Eleazar b. Azariah, for it has been taught:

[G]   There is the case of R. Eleazar b. Azariah and R. Aqiba on a ship. R. Aqiba built a *sukkah* on the bow of the ship, and the wind came and blew it off. Said to him R. Eleazar b. Azariah,

"Aqiba, now where is your *sukkah*?" [Eleazar maintained that it was not an appropriate place for a *sukkah*, because the boat was moving and not at rest. Thus all three take the same view of a moving beast or vehicle. It is subject to a different set of laws from what is at rest.]

[III.A] [At issue is M. Er. 3:3A–C:] *[If] one put it into a tree—[If] it is above ten handbreadths, his* erub *is not a valid* erub. *[If he put it] below ten handbreadths, his* erub *is a valid* erub. [The *erub* must lie within the control of the person for whom it establishes a Sabbath residence. It also must lie in public domain, so that the person relying upon the *erub* has access to it (at least in theory). The problem of A–C, therefore, is simple. The area of the tree above ten handbreadths is private domain, that below is neutral domain (*karmelit*), neither private nor public. If the *erub* is above ten handbreadths, in the foliage of the tree, then, when sun sets and the *erub* acquires a place for the man, the man himself has not got access to the *erub*, which is not in public domain but in private property. So he could not at that moment climb up the tree and get at the token meal. The man must be able to get at the *erub* and eat it. He cannot do so—so it is no *erub*.] *Lo, this is a valid* erub *[M. Er. 3:3C]* **but it is forbidden to carry it about [since he may not climb the tree to get at it]. If it was located three handbreadths from the ground, it is permitted [to carry it about] [T. Er. 2:13].**

[B] Now here is the question:

[C] If the *erub* is valid, it should be permitted to carry it about, and if it is not permitted to carry it about, then it should not be a valid *erub*.

[D] [The prohibition against climbing a tree to get at the *erub* is merely by reason of the general laws on Sabbath rest, which include the one against making use of the tree on that day.] Indeed, it would be appropriate for him to violate the restrictions governing Sabbath rest [and to utilize the tree by climbing it, and so to] eat the *erub*.

[E] If that is the case, then even if the *erub* is higher than ten handbreadths, it should be valid in all regards.

[F] R. Judah in the name of Samuel: "Interpret the Mishnah to speak of a case in which the beam of the tree was four handbreadths [thus forming a domain unto itself, which one may not enter]. [The tree thus constitutes private domain. One may not carry from the tree to the public domain.]"

[G] Said R. Mana, "And the rule then applies to a case in which the public domain completely surrounds the tree on all sides [for the reason clear from F],

[H] "and in the case of one who says, 'Let my place of spending the Sabbath be beneath the tree.' [The man is in public domain, the tree in private.]"

[I] It has been taught: "**[If he put it] within three handbreadths, it is permitted to handle it.**

[J] "**[If] he put it into a basket and hung it in a tree above ten handbreadths, his *erub* is not valid.**

[K] "**[If he hung the basket] lower than ten handbreadths, his *erub* is valid.**

[L] "**And it is prohibited to handle it," the words of Rabbi [T. Er. 2:13D–F].**

[M] If he put it lower than three handbreadths, it is permitted to do so.

[N] Now here is the question:

[O] If the *erub* is valid, it should be permitted to carry it about, and if it is not permitted to carry it about, then it should not be a valid *erub*.

[P] R. Aha in the name of R. Hinena: "It is suitable to turn the basket on its side and [without detaching it from the tree] [53a] nullifying the private domain that is represented by that basket]. [The man may get at the *erub* without carrying it from one domain to another by inclining the basket.]"

[Q] Said R. Yose, "That is to say that in the case of a bench which one set in the public domain, ten handbreadths high and four broad, since one may turn it over and thereby nullify it as private domain,

[R] ["if one set an *erub* on such a bench], his *erub* is valid, and it is permitted to carry it about [by analogy to the case of the basket]."

[S] There we have learned: *If two sides of a sukkah are formed by a tree, and one is made by man, or two are made by man and one*

is formed by a tree, it is valid. But they do not go up into that
sukkah *on the festival day [M. 2:4E–H].*

[T]   Now here you said that [the *sukkah*] is valid, but they do not go
        up into it on the festival day. Now here you have said that the
        erub is valid, and that it is permitted to carry it about [in line
        with P]. [But does a person not utilize the tree on the Sabbath or
        festival, if he follows Aha's instructions at P? Why is it forbid-
        den to use the *sukkah* leaning on a tree on the festival or Sab-
        bath, but permitted in regard to reaching the *erub*?]

[U]   Said R. Jeremiah, "Here [with regard to the *sukkah*], one has set
        the *sukkah* above [in the branches, and one has to climb the tree
        to get to the *sukkah*, built as a tree house]. [That is forbidden.]
        There [with regard to the basket], one reaches out to the basket
        from below, [and does not have to climb the tree to get at it]."

[V]   [In accord with Jeremiah's reasoning, we may] derive a rule from
        that case for this one, and a rule from this case for that one.

[W]   We may derive a rule from this case for that one: If the basket
        was located in the side of the tree, the *erub* is valid, and it is
        permitted to carry it about [since one has got access to it, for it
        is in the side of the tree, not in the tree itself].

[X]   And a rule may be derived from that case for the present one: If
        there were two poles protruding [from a tree], and one spread
        sukkah-roofing on them, it is a valid *sukkah,* and it is permitted
        to enter it on the festival [since one enters the *sukkah* without
        climbing the tree, and that is permissible, in line with the con-
        ception of Aha at P].

[Y]   Said R. Yose, "[It is not sound to assign one case to the edge of
        the tree branches, the other to the center of the foliage. Rather:]
        both that case and this one deal with the side of the tree's [boughs,
        and not the center]. [That is, both the *sukkah* and the basket are
        located in such wise as to be accessible without climbing the tree.]

[Z]   "Then how shall we interpret the problem [dealt with by Jeremiah
        at U]?

[AA]   "It is in accord with R. Jacob bar Aha in the name of R. Zeira:
        'It represents the view of R. Simon b. Eleazar.'

[BB]   "For R. Simeon b. Eleazar says, 'It is permitted to make use of
        the sides of a beast on the Sabbath.'

[CC]   "And the same rule applies to the sides of a beast as to the sides of a tree." [The contradiction between the rules is resolved more elegantly when we simply declare that what is hanging from the side of a tree, or a *sukkah* located at the side of the tree and not as a tree house, may be utilized on the Sabbath or a festival, in which case M. 2:4 will not accord with Simeon b. Eleazar as read by Zeira-Yose.]

The operative principle is that one may not make use of a tree or a camel on the festival day (M. Bes. 5:2). The restrictions then are the same as they are on the Sabbath. The contrast between M. 2:4A–B and C–D is therefore quite clear. E–L then form a secondary expansion of the same point as is made about C. If the *sukkah* depends upon the tree, then it may not be used on the festival day. If it stands on its own and does not depend on the tree, then it may be used on the festival, as M. 2:4K–L explain. Unit **I** presents a simple explanation of the ambiguous circumstance to which M. refers. Unit **II** presents three authorities who will not concur with M. 2:4A, and further signals that M. represents the position of Aqiba. Unit **III** is joined not merely because it intersects with M. at the point at which M. 2:4 is cited. Rather, it raises essentially the problem operative at M. 2:4E–L, namely, utilizing a tree on the festival day. The issue now is phrased in terms of locating an *erub*—a symbolic meal establishing a Sabbath residence different from the one of a town in general—in a tree, and the consequences of doing so. Getting at the *erub* then is the problem; if one is prohibited from utilizing the tree, e.g., climbing it, he may not get at the *erub* and hence he may not carry it about. (PM's interpretation here introduces issues I believe not essential in the interpretation of the Talmud.)

2:5

[A]   *He who makes his* sukkah *among trees, and the trees are its sides—it is valid.*

[B]   *Agents engaged in a religious duty are exempt from the requirement of dwelling in a* sukkah.

[C]   *Sick folk and those who serve them are exempt from the requirement of dwelling in a* sukkah.

[D]   *[People] eat and drink in a random manner outside of a* sukkah.

[I.A]   [As to M. 2:5B:] R. Hunah went to Ein Tab for the sanctification of the New Moon. [He thus was engaged in a religious
duty.] As he was going along, he became thirsty while on the
road, but he did not agree to taste a thing until he had entered
the shade of the *sukkah* of R. Yohanan, the scribe of Gopta.

[B]   [As to M. 2:5C,] said R. Mana, "It is not the end of the matter
that those who are so sick as to be dying [and those who serve
them] are exempt. But even those who are sick but in no danger
are exempt [cf. T. 2:2B–C].

[C]   It has been taught [in T.'s version]: **Said Rabban Simeon b.
Gamaliel, "MᶜSH W: I had a pain in the eye in Caesarion, and
R. Yose b. Rabbi permitted me to sleep, along with my ser-
vant, outside of the** *sukkah*" [T. Suk. 2:2D].

[D]   R. Ba bar Zabeda said, "The groomsmen and all who share in
the marriage-canopy are exempt from the religious duty of dwelling in the *sukkah*."

[II.A]   It has been taught: [In T.'s version:] **City guards by day are
exempt from the religious requirement of dwelling in a** *sukkah*
by day, but they are liable by night.

[B]   **City guards by night are exempt from the religious requirement of dwelling in a** *sukkah* **by night, but they are liable
by day.**

[C]   **City guards by day and by night are exempt from the religious
requirement of dwelling in a** *sukkah* **by day and by night
[T. Suk. 2:3C–E].**

[D]   That which you have said applies to guards against invasion. But
as to guards of money, they have treated them as equivalent to
the guards of fields and orchards.

[E]   Abodema of Milha was sleeping before his stall. R. Hiyya bar Ba
came by and said to him, "Go, sleep in your *sukkah*."

[F]   R. Mana was the groomsman of R. Jacob bar Paliti. He came
and asked R. Yose, who said to him, "Go, sleep in your *sukkah*."

[G]   R. Isaac bar Marion was the groomsman of a certain man. He
asked R. Eleazar, who said to him, "Go, sleep in your *sukkah*."

[III.A]   **MᶜSH B: R. Ilai went to R. Eliezer in Lud. He said to him,
"Now what's going on, Ilai? Are you not among those who**

observe the festival? Have they not said that it is not praiseworthy of a person to leave his home on a festival? For it is
said, 'And you will rejoice on your festival'" (Deut. 16:14) [T.
Suk. 2:1C].

[B]   There is the following: R. Zeirah went to the circumcision of [a
son of] R. Ila, and he did not agree to taste a thing.

[C]   We do not know [the reason, that is,] whether it was because it
was not his custom to eat a thing until he had prayed the Additional Prayer [on the festival], or whether it was because it is not
praiseworthy for a disciple of sages to leave his home on a festival and to go along.

[IV.A]   [As to M. 2:5D:] Said R. Eleazar, "There is such a thing as a
random meal [that may be taken outside of a *sukkah*], but there
is no such thing as random sleep. [All sleeping must be in the
sukkah.]"

[B]   [Giving Eleazar's reason] associates say, "For someone sinks into
sleep."

[C]   Said R. Ila, "For a man may sleep only a few winks and that is
enough [sleeping for him, so it is never random]."

[D]   What is the practical difference among these various reasons?

[E]   Giving someone else wake-up instructions:

[F]   In the view of associates, it is permitted to [sleep outside a *sukkah*
if one does so, since that will take account of their concern].

[G]   In the view of R. Ila it is forbidden [to sleep outside a *sukkah*,
even if one tells someone else to wake him up, because that brief
sleep may suffice and hence will not be considered random].

The Talmud takes up M.'s themes and complements them in fa-
miliar ways, both providing amplification for M. and also citing
T.'s pertinent materials.

2:6

[A]   M'SH W: *They brought Rabban Yohanan b. Zakkai some cooked
food to taste, and to Rabban Gamaliel two dates and a dipper of
water.*

[B]   *And they said, "Bring them up to the sukkah."*

[C]   *And when they gave to R. Sadoq food less than an egg's bulk, he took it in a cloth and ate it outside of the sukkah and said no blessing after it.*

[I.A]   [With reference to M. 2:6,] they theorized that *he did not say a blessing after it [M. 2:6C]* means that he did not say the three complete blessings, but lo, he did say an abbreviated version.

[B]   The following has been taught: He did not say one blessing, nor did he say three.

[II.A]   It has been taught: In the case of any food, after which they say three blessings—before it they say, "Who brings forth bread from the earth."

[B]   In the case of any food after which they do not say three blessings—before it they do not say, "Who brings forth bread from the earth."

[C]   They objected, "Lo, there is the case of eating food in less than the volume of an olive's bulk. They do not say three blessings over such food. Now if that is the case, they also should not say before eating it, 'Who brings forth bread from the earth.'"

[D]   R. Jacob bar Aha said, "It was in regard to other kinds of foods that the cited passage [II.A–B] is required."

Unit **I** clarifies M. 2:6C. Unit **II** is attached because it is relevant to unit **I**.

2:7

[A]   *R. Eliezer says, "Fourteen meals is a person obligated to eat in the sukkah,*

[B]   *"one by day and one by night."*

[C]   *And sages say, "There is no fixed requirement, except for the first two nights of the Festival alone."*

[D]   *And further did R. Eliezer say, "He who has not eaten his meal in the sukkah on the first night of the Festival should make up for it on the last night of the Festival."*

[E]   *And sages say, "there is no way of making it up.*

[F]   *"Concerning such a case it is said, 'That which is crooked cannot be made straight, and that which is wanting cannot be reckoned'" (Qoh. 1:15).*

[I.A]   What is the Scriptural basis for the position of R. Eliezer?

[B]   In reference to the *sukkah*, it is said, ". . . you will dwell . . ." (Lev. 23:42).

[C]   And elsewhere it is said, "At the door of the tent of meeting you shall dwell day and night for seven days, performing what the Lord has charged, lest you die; for so I am commanded" (Lev. 8:35).

[D]   Just as the case of "dwelling" stated there indicates that the nights are equivalent to the days, so dwelling here indicates that the nights are equivalent to the days, [hence the rule of M. 2:7B].

[E]   [As to the reason of sages,] R. Yohanan in the name of R. Ishmael: "'Fifteenth [of the month]' (Lev. 23:6) is stated with regard to Passover, and 'Fifteenth [of the month]' (Lev. 23:34) is stated with regard to the Festival. Just as the fifteenth stated with reference to Passover speaks of the first night as obligatory and the other days as optional [in respect to eating unleavened bread], so the fifteenth stated with regard to the Festival indicates that [sitting in the *sukkah*] on the first night is obligatory, and on all other days is optional."

[F]   Associates asked, "Do we then say, 'Just as in the case of the Passover seder, one must eat the unleavened bread with a ravenous appetite, so here one must enter the *sukkah* with a ravenous appetite'?"

[G]   R. Zeirah asked, "Do we further say that in regard to the unleavened bread on Passover, one must eat an olive's bulk of unleavened bread, and so here, one must eat an olive's bulk of grain in a *sukkah*?"

[H]   R. Hoshaiah said, "All seven days are obligatory. [One must sit or dwell in the *sukkah* every day of the festival.]"

[I]   R. Berekhiah said, "There is a dispute on that matter."

[J]   R. Abona said, "There is no dispute on that matter.

[K]   "What R. Yohanan has said [E] [that the first night alone is obligatory] applies when a person has had the intention [of fulfilling his obligation on the first night].

[L]   "What R. Hoshaiah said [H] applies when one has not formed the intention [of fulfilling his obligation on the first night]."

[II.A]   [With reference to M. 2:7D:] It has been taught in the name of R. Eliezer, "He who did not make his *sukkah* on the eve of the Festival should not make it on the Festival itself."

[B]   And did not Bar Qappara teach, "If one's *sukkah* fell down on the Festival, he may set it up on the Festival"?

[C]   R. Aha in the name of R. Hinena: "It is a penalty that R. Eliezer has imposed upon him who did not make his *sukkah* on the eve of the Festival."

[III.A]   The opinions assigned to R. Eliezer are contradictory.

[B]   There he has said, *"Fourteen meals is a person obligated to eat in the* sukkah*" [M. 2:7A]*, and here he has said this [that if one did not eat on the first night in the *sukkah*, he makes it up on the last night]. [But on the last night there is no *sukkah* any longer. It is no longer obligatory to eat there.]

[C]   Said R. Aha, "As to carrying out the religious duty, [Eliezer and sages] are in agreement [that the religious duty applies only to the first night of the Festival, and, consequently, Eliezer concurred that it is merely a religious deed, but not an obligation, to eat the other meals in the *sukkah* (PM)]."

Unit I provides a scriptural basis for M. 2:7A–C's two positions. Since Passover and the Festival are treated by sages as analogous to one another, a series of rather comical questions are generated, I.E–F. Then the issue of whether or not the first night alone is obligatory is taken up. Unit II clarifies the conflict of two rulings. Unit III compares Eliezer's view at M. 2:7A–B and M. 2:7D and harmonizes Eliezer's views at both places by bringing Eliezer over to sages' position in the former case.

2:8

[A]   *He whose head and the greater part of whose body are in the* sukkah, *but whose table is in the house—*

[B]   *the House of Shammai declare invalid.*

[C]   *And the House of Hillel declare valid.*

[D]   *Said the House of Hillel to the House of Shammai, "Was not the precedent so, that the elders of the House of Shammai and the elders of the House of Hillel went along to pay a sick-call on R. Yohanan b. Hahorani, and they found him sitting with his head and the greater part of his body in the sukkah, and his table in the house, and they said nothing at all to him!"*

[E]   *Said the House of Shammai to them, "Is there proof from that story? But in point of fact they did say to him, 'If this is how you act, you have never in your whole life fulfilled the religious requirement of dwelling in a sukkah!'"*

[I.A]   It is not the end of the matter [from the viewpoint of the House of Shammai] that the whole table be in the house. Even if only part of it is there, [it is invalid].

[B]   How much would part of the table be? A handbreadth.

[II.A] [With reference to M. Ter. 5:4, which follows (in the translation of Alan Peck, *Terumot*, pp. 170–71): *A seah of unclean heave-offering which fell into a hundred seahs of clean heave-offering—the House of Shammai declare (the mixture) forbidden (for consumption by a priest), but the House of Hillel permit. Said the House of Hillel to the House of Shammai, "Since clean (heave-offering) is forbidden to nonpriests, and unclean (heave-offering) is forbidden to priests, if clean (heave-offering) can be neutralized, so unclean (heave-offering) can be neutralized." Said to them the House of Shammai, "No! If unconsecrated produce, to which leniency applies and which is permitted to nonpriests, neutralizes clean (heave-offering), should heave-offering, to which stringency applies and which is forbidden to nonpriests, (have that same power and) neutralize unclean (heave-offering)?" After they had agreed: R. Eliezer says, "Let it be raised up and burned." But sages say, "It has been lost through its scantiness":]* R. Judah bar Pazzi and R. Aibu bar Nigri were in session, saying, "We have learned: *After they had agreed.*

[B]   "Who agreed with whom? Was it the House of Shammai with the view of the House of Hillel, or the House of Hillel with the position of the House of Shammai?"

[C]   They said, "Let us go out and learn [what others may know about the matter], and they heard R. Hezekiah, R. Aha in the name of R. Judah b. Levi [state], 'We have heard that the House of Shammai accepted the view of the House of Hillel only in regard to this matter alone.'"

[D]   R. Huna in the name of R. Aibu: "The Mishnah has made that same point: *He who pours from jar to jar, and a Tebul Yom touched the stream of liquid—if there is in the jar any wine, the wine he touched is neutralized in a mixture of one hundred and one [M. T.Y. 2:7E–F].*

[E]   "If you maintain that the House of Hillel accepted the position of the House of Shammai, then the wine should not be neutralized [just as the House of Shammai do not accept the principle of neutralization at the cited passage of M. Ter. 5:4]."

[F]   [Rejecting this view,] Who taught here, "It may be neutralized"? It is neither the House of Hillel nor the House of Shammai.

[G]   Said R. Idi, "We may say that the House of Hillel is responsible for the framing of this tradition, prior to the House of Shammai's concession to them."

[H]   Said R. Yose, "The Mishnah has made that very point: *After they had agreed: R. Eliezer says, 'Let it be raised up and burned.'* Now was not R. Eliezer himself a member of the House of Shammai?"

[I]   [Concurring in Yose's view,] said R. Hinenah, "The Tannaitic tradition has made the same point: 'After these had agreed [53b] with those, it may be neutralized [just as the Hillelites insist].'"

[J]   Now is it possible that the House of Shammai should win the argument, and then concur with the opinion of [the House of Hillel (as H–I claim)]?

[K]   Said R. Abun, "There is the possibility of yet another reply here, in line with what R. Hoshaiah taught [in T.'s version]:

[L]   **'And is it not an argument *a minori ad majus*? If in a case in which Torah was stringent, that of nonpriests who eat heave-offering, lo, [the heave-offering] is neutralized in unconsecrated produce [and then] eaten by nonpriests, in a case in which Torah is lenient, that of priests who eat heave-offering, is it not logical that [the heave-offering] is neutralized in (correct to read:) heave-offering [and then] is eaten by priests?'** [T. Ter. 6:4J (Peck, p. 179)]."

[III.A]   Why did the House of Hillel have the merit that the law should be decided in accord with their views?

[B]   Said R. Judah bar Pazzi, "Because they put the words of the House of Shammai before their words.

[C]   "Not only so, but they occasionally accepted the opinion of the House of Shammai and retracted theirs."

[D]   R. Simon bar Zabeda objected before R. Ila, "Perhaps we should say that it was the Tannaitic framer of the traditions who saw that [the House of Shammai] were the elders of the two and so placed their opinion first [vs. B]?

[E]   "And lo, it has been taught: *Was not the precedent so, that the elders of the House of Shammai and the elders of the House of Hillel went along to pay a sick-call on R. Yohanan b. Hahorani [M. 2:8D].*

[F]   "Should it not be said, 'Our elders and your elders'? [Hence it was the Tannaitic framer of the tradition, and not the House of Hillel itself, who placed the opinion of the House of Shammai first.]"

[IV.A]   Said R. Zeirah, R. Hunah in the name of Rab: "The law accords with the position of the House of Shammai [at M. 2:8]."

[B]   R. Jeremiah, R. Samuel bar R. Isaac in the name of Rab: "Since the House of Shammai drove off the House of Hillel [who had no reply to M. 2:8E], it follows that the law is in accord with their opinion."

Unit **I** clarifies the position of the House of Shammai. Units **II–IV** serve Y. Ter. 5:4 and make no contribution to the discussion of our tractate.

2:9

[A]   *Women, slaves, and minors are exempt from the religious requirement of dwelling in a sukkah.*

[B]   *A minor who can take care of himself is liable to the religious requirement of dwelling in a sukkah.*

[C]   *M^cSH W: Shammai the Elder's daughter-in-law gave birth, and he broke away some of the plaster and covered the whole with sukkah-roofing over her bed, on account of the infant.*

[I.A]   What is the definition of a minor [at M. 2 : 9B]?

[B]   A member of the House of Yannai said, "It is any who has to have his mother wipe him."

[C]   R. Yohanan said, "It is any who wakes up at night and calls out, 'Mommy.'"

[D]   R. Hoshaiah taught: "*A minor who can take care of himself is liable to the religious requirement of dwelling in a sukkah [M. 2 : 9B]*, but he nonetheless carries out his obligation [in regard to carrying on the Sabbath] in relying upon the *erub* prepared by his mother."

The Talmud clarifies M. 2 : 9B.

2:10

A]   *All seven days a person treats his sukkah as his regular dwelling and his house as his sometime-dwelling.*

[B]   *[If] it began to rain, at what point is it permitted to empty out [the sukkah]?*

[C]   *From the point at which the porridge will spoil.*

[D]   *They made a parable: To what is the matter comparable?*

[E]   *To a slave who came to mix a cup of wine for his master, and his master threw the flagon into his face.*

[I.A]   It is written, "You shall dwell in booths for seven days; all that are native in Israel shall dwell in booths" (Lev. 23 : 42).

[B]   And there is no "dwelling" except in the sense of "living permanently."

[C]   That is in line with the following verse: "When you come to the land which the Lord your God gives you, and you possess it and dwell in it, and then say, 'I will set a king over me, like all the nations that are round about me'" (Deut. 17 : 14).

[D]   "Dwelling" in the *sukkah* means that one should eat in the *sukkah,* walk about in the *sukkah,* and move his goods up into the *sukkah.*

[**II**.A]   *If it began to rain, at what point is it permitted to empty out the* sukkah? *From the point at which the porridge will spoil [M. 2:9B–C].*

[B]   It is not the end of the matter that the porridge must actually spoil.

[C]   But even if it rained enough so as to spoil porridge [even if it did not actually spoil], [that suffices].

[D]   It is not the end of the matter that it is a porridge of grits. But a porridge of anything at all [falls under the same rule].

[E]   It has been taught: Just as they may empty out the *sukkah* on account of rain, so that may be done on account of heat or mosquitoes.

[**III**.A]   Rabban Gamaliel would go in and out all night long.

[B]   R. Eliezer would go in and out all night long.

[C]   A disciple of R. Mana instructed one of the relatives of the patriarch, "If one has gone out [because of mosquitoes, for example,] they do not trouble the person to go back in."

[D]   Did this disciple not hear that Rabban Gamaliel would go in and out all night long, [and] R. Eliezer would go in and go out all night long?

Unit **I** provides a scriptural proof for M. 2:9A. Unit **II** amplifies M. 2:9B–C. Unit **III** answers the question of whether, if one has had to leave, he goes back into the *sukkah* later on.

3:1

[A] [53c] *A stolen or dried up palm branch is invalid.*

[B] *And one deriving from an* asherah *or an apostate town in invalid.*

[C] *[If] its tip was broken off, or [if] its leaves were split, it is invalid.*

[D] *[If] its leaves were spread apart, it is valid.*

[E] *R. Judah says, "Let him tie it up at the end."*

[F] *Thorn-palms of the Iron Mountain are valid.*

[G] *Any palm branch which is [only] three handbreaths long,*

[H] *sufficient to shake,*

[I] *is valid.*

[I.A] [Explaining why a stolen palm branch is invalid,] R. Hiyya taught, "'And you shall take for yourselves [on the first day the fruit of goodly trees, branches of palm trees, and boughs of leafy trees, and willows of the brook]' (Lev. 23:40). The meaning is that they must be yours and not stolen."

[B] Said R. Levi, "This one who takes a stolen palm branch—to what is he comparable?

[C] "To one who pays respect to the ruler by bringing him a [gold] dish, and it turns out to belong to the ruler himself."

[D] They said, "Woe for this one, who turns his advocate into his critic!"

[**II**.A]   [As to M. 3:1B, One deriving from an apostate town:] A ram's horn belonging to a Temple of idolatry, or one belonging to an apostate town—

[B]   R. Eleazar said, "It is valid."

[C]   R. Hiyya taught, "It is valid."

[D]   R. Hoshaiah taught, "It is invalid."

[E]   All concur in the case of a palm branch [deriving from such a source] that it is invalid.

[F]   What is the difference between a ram's horn and a palm branch?

[G]   Said R. Yose, "In the case of a palm branch, it is written, 'And you shall take for yourselves [on the first day the fruit of goodly trees, branches of palm trees, and boughs of leafy trees, and willows of the brook]' (Lev. 23:40). The meaning is that it must belong to you, and it must not be in the category of what may not be used for your benefit.

[H]   "But here it is written, 'On the first day of the seventh month you shall have a holy convocation; you shall do no laborious work. It is a day for you to blow the trumpets' (Num. 29:1). The trumpets may derive from any source [since no qualifying language is inserted]."

[I]   [Offering a different point of differentiation,] said R. Eleazar, "There it is with the body of the object itself that one carries out the obligation. But here [in the case of the horn], it is merely with the sound that it makes. And can a sound be declared prohibited for one's benefit? [Surely not.]"

[**III**.A]   What is at issue [**I**.A–D, between Hiyya's and Levi's explanations]?

[B]   If one stole a branch that had already been planed [for use on the festival].

[C]   But if one stole the branch and then planed it himself [so acquiring it by changing its character permanently], then all the thief owes the original owner is money [on which both parties concur].

[**IV**.A]   If one stole a palm branch from one source, myrtle from a second, and a willow from yet a third and then he bound the three together into a bunch, [what is the law]?

[B]   Let us derive the answer from the following:

[C]   As to a *sukkah* that has been stolen—

[D]   there is a Tanna who teaches that it is valid.

[E]   There is a Tanna who teaches that it is invalid.

[F]   R. Simeon in the name of R. Joshua b. Levi: "He who has said that it is valid maintains that view when one has stolen the ground [on which he built the *sukkah*]. [The ground is never regarded as stolen, since there is no substantial change made to it, so the thief never effects ownership. Consequently, the *sukkah* is regarded as one that is merely borrowed from the land-owner, and it is valid.]

[G]   "The one who has said that it is invalid deals with a case in which he stole the roofing. [In this case the thief has effected ownership of what he has stolen. In the case of the question we have raised, no permanent change has been made in the character of what has been stolen. Consequently, the thief does not effect ownership of the materials, and the branch, myrtle, and willow do not serve to fulfill his obligation.]"

[H]   But it is not possible that he will not tie them together [and so change their character].

[I]   We deal with a case in which he holds them side by side at the top [but does not do anything to them, in line with the reasoning spelled out at F].

[J]   [As to the stolen *sukkah*,] rabbis of Caesarea in the name of R. Yohanan [differing from the picture of C–G]: "In the opinion of both parties the *sukkah* that is stolen is invalid.

[K]   "What is the definition of a stolen *sukkah*?

[L]   "It is one entered by one's fellow without his knowledge and consent."

[M]   This is illustrated by the following:

[N]   Gamaliel Zuga made a *sukkah* in the marketplace. R. Simeon b. Laqish came by and said to him, "Who gave you permission [to build it here]?"

[V.A] *A dried up one is invalid* [M. 3:1A].

[B]   R. Abin in the name of R. Judah bar Pazzi: "A dried up one is invalid, in line with the following verse of Scripture: 'The dead do not praise the Lord, nor do any that go down into silence'" (Ps. 115:17).

[C]   It has been taught in the name of R. Judah, "A dried up one itself is valid" [cf. T. Suk. 2:9].

[D]   Said to them R. Judah, "And is it not so that in the sea ports they hand on their palm branches to their children as inheritances?"

[E]   They said to him, "They do not derive the law from what is done under duress."

[VI.A]   They asked before R. Abina, "If the ends of the *lulab* dried up, what is the law?"

[B]   [Rethinking this question, they asked,] "What would be the difference between the ends and the body of the branch? [Surely if the latter is invalid when dried up, so the former will be invalid when dried up.]"

[C]   He said to them, "[No, there is a difference,] for the one is comely, and the other is not comely."

[VII.A]   R. Malokh in the name of R. Joshua b. Levi: "If the central rib of a branch of palm leaves was divided, it is in the status of its leaves being spread apart [and valid, in line with M. 3:1D]."

[VIII.A]   As to palm branches [Lev. 23:40]—

[B]   R. Tarfon says, "They must be bunches of palms."

[C]   R. Aqiba says, "Palm branches as their name implies."

[D]   R. Judah says, "If it is separated, he should tie it together."

[IX.A]   What are the thorn-palms of the Iron Mountain that are valid [M. 3:1F]?

[B]   It is any, the head of which touches the side of the root of that.

[X.A]   It has been taught: If a palm branch is dried up, it is invalid.

[B]   If it merely appears to be dried up, it is valid.

[C]   R. Simeon bar Abba in the name of R. Yohanan: "That is precisely the meaning of the Mishnah:

[D]   *"Sufficient to shake—it is valid [M. 3:1H–I]."*

[XI.A]   It has been taught: **A myrtle and a willow are to be three hand-breadths long, and a palm branch, four.**

[B]   It has been taught: "**It is measured with a cubit of five hand-breadths,**" the words of R. Tarfon. [T. Suk. 2:8B–C.]

[C]   But sages say, "With a cubit of six handbreadths."

[D]   In the view of R. Tarfon, they make use of wide handbreadths, and in the opinion of sages they make use of narrow handbreadths.

[XII.A]   R. Jonah and R. Simeon b. Laqish in the name of R. Judah the Patriarch: "A palm branch is to be a handbreadth in length."

[B]   R. Simeon in the name of R. Joshua b. Levi: "The hyssop must be a handbreadth in length."

[C]   R. Zeirah asked, "Will a palm branch be a handbreadth and a hyssop also be a handbreadth?"

[D]   Said R. Yose, R. Simon explained this matter, R. Hinena, R. Simon in the name of R. Joshua b. Levi: "A palm branch must be a handbreadth in length. A hyssop must be a hand-breadth in length. A ram's horn must be a handbreadth in length. An afterbirth [to be subject to the law] is a handbreadth in length."

[E]   And some say, "Also the third side of the *sukkah* may be merely a handbreadth in height."

[F]   R. Zeira raised the question: "When we say a palm branch must be a handbreadth in length, is that exclusive of the backbone? Likewise with the hyssop, is that exclusive of the berries?"

[G]   R. Yose, R. Tabi in the name of Rab, R. Hinena, R. Parnakh, R. Mattenah, Yose bar Menassia in the name of Rab: "A palm branch must be a handbreadth in length, exclusive of the back-bone. A hyssop must be a handbreadth in length, exclusive of the berries."

The Talmud systematically works its way through M.'s materials, providing a brief exegesis for each one, and raising some theoretical questions as well. Its principal interest is in M. 3:1A, the stolen palm branch, and hence, the other stolen items. Unit **I** provides a scriptural basis for this rule, and unit **II** differentiates the present item from another, not subject to the stated restriction, also on the basis of scriptural exegesis. Units **III** and **IV** enter into the question of the theory of theft, asking why an object is alienated from its owner. The first thesis is that when the thief permanently changes the character of the object, he has acquired it. It then becomes his. Yohanan, **IV**.J, rejects this theorizing altogether. Units **V–VIII** and **X** concentrate on the matter of the dried up palm branch. Unit **IX** addresses M. 3:1F. Units **XI** and **XII** deal with the required length of the objects under discussion here as well as other objects, that is, M. 3:1G–I.

3:2

[A]   *A stolen or dried up myrtle branch is invalid.*

[B]   *And one deriving from an asherah or an apostate town is invalid.*

[C]   *[If] its tip was broken off, [or if] its leaves were split,*

[D]   *or if its berries were more numerous than its leaves,*

[E]   *it is invalid.*

[F]   *But if one then removed some of them, it is valid.*

[G]   *And they do not remove [some of them] on the festival day.*

[I.A]   It is written, "[And you shall take on the first day the fruit of goodly trees, branches of palm trees, and] boughs of leafy trees, [and willows of the brook; and you shall rejoice before the Lord your God seven days]" (Lev. 23:40).

[B]   The requirement is that the branches cover the larger part of it and resemble a chain, and what is such a tree? It is a myrtle.

[C]   If you say that an olive resembles a chain, still, its branches do not cover the larger part of it.

[D]   If you say that, in the case of a *zargunah*-tree, its branches cover the larger part of it, still, it does not resemble a chain.

[E]   [What is the tree that meets the stated requirement?] It is a myrtle.

[II.A]   Hiyya bar Ada in the name of R. Yohanan: "[As to M. 3:2D, If the berries were more numerous than the leaves, it is invalid,] this has been taught in the case of black ones."

[B]   Why should it be invalid?

[C]   Is it because they are not the same color as the wood [since the wood is green, the berries black]?

[D]   Or is it because the fruit is ripe [and scripture wants the boughs, not the fruit, to be waved]?

[E]   What is the practical difference between these reasons?

[F]   A tree which produced green boughs.

[G]   If the operative reason is that they are not similar to the wood, lo, these are not of the same color as the wood.

[H]   But the reason can only be because the fruit is now ripe [so even green ones would be valid].

Unit **I** explains the choice of the myrtle, M. 3:2A, and unit **II** amplifies M. 3:2D.

3:3

[A]   *A stolen or dried up willow branch is invalid.*

[B]   *And one deriving from an* asherah *or an apostate town is invalid.*

[C]   *[If] its tip was broken off, [if] its leaves split, or [if it was] a mountain willow,*

[D]   *it is invalid.*

[E]   *[If] it was shriveled, or [if] some of the leaves dropped off,*

[F]   *or [if it came] from a [naturally watered] field [and did not grow by a brook],*

[G]   *it is valid.*

[I.A]   It is written, "Willows of the brook" (Lev. 23:40).

[B]   I know only that I may use willows that grow by a brook. How do I know that I may use willows that grow in a field that is watered by rain or a field in the mountains?

[C]   Scripture says, "And willows. . . ."

[D]   Abba Saul says, "[The use of the plural for] willows of the brook indicates that two separate purposes are served by willows. There

is a willow to be included in the palm branch [*lulab*], and there
is a willow to be used in the Temple."

[E]   [Reverting to I.A–C,] if so, why is it said, "Willows of the brook"
[if B is correct that willows growing under other circumstances
arc acccptable]?

[F]   That is meant to exclude the kind that grows in a waterless region.

[G]   **What is the kind that grows in waterless regions?**

[H]   One that has teeth like a sickle is valid.

[I]   **One that has teeth like a saw** [T. Suk. 2 : 7F–G] is invalid.

[J]   **What is a valid willow branch? One which has a red stem and
an elongated leaf.**

[K]   **What is an invalid willow branch? One which has a white stem
and a round leaf [T. Suk. 2 : 7].**

The Talmud defines the suitable willow branch and resorts to
Scripture to prove its case.

3 : 4

[A]   *R. Ishmael says, "Three myrtle branches, two willow branches,
one palm branch, and one citron [are required],*

[B]   *"even if two [of the myrtle branches] have their tips broken off,
and only one does not have its tip broken off."*

[C]   *R. Tarfon says, "Even if all three of them have their tips broken
off, [they are valid]."*

[D]   *R. Aqiba says, "Just as one palm branch and one citron [are
required], so one myrtle branch and one willow branch [are
required]."*

[I.A]   [With reference to Lev. 23 : 40: "And you shall take on the first
day the fruit of goodly trees, branches of palm trees, boughs
of leafy trees, and willows of the brook,"] R. Ishmael provided
the following exegesis [in support of his position at M. 3 : 4A]:
" 'The fruit of goodly trees' refers to a single piece of fruit.
'Branches of palm trees' refers to a single such branch. 'Boughs

of leafy trees' refers to three boughs of myrtle. 'Willows of the brook' refers to two willows.

[B]   "Two trained [myrtle branches], and one which does not have its tip cut off."

[C]   *R. Tarfon says, "Even if all three of them have their tips broken off, they are valid" [M. 3:4C].*

[D]   R. Ba bar Mamel raised the following question before R. Imi: "Just as R. Ishmael requires several myrtle branches, should he [not] require several examples of each of the other species?"

[E]   He said to him, "Do you think that, so far as R. Ishmael is concerned, if the tip is cut off, it falls into the category of goodly [trees]? [In fact, he requires only one example of the species.]

[F]   "And lo, we have learned: *R. Tarfon says, 'Even if all three of them have their tips broken off. . . .'*

[G]   "Now a person does not say, 'Even . . . ,' unless he concurs with what has gone before. [That indicates that Ishmael has said a single valid example alone is what is required.]"

[H]   Said R. Haggai, asking his question before R. Yose, "What does R. Tarfon come to add to what R. Ishmael has said?"

[I]   [53d] He said to him, "R. Ishmael does not hold the opinion that one with the tip cut off falls into the category of a goodly tree, while R. Tarfon maintains that one with the tip cut off does fall into the category of a goodly tree."

[II.A]   R. Yose: When he came here [to the Land of Israel] he saw people choosing the correct myrtle.

[B]   He said to them, "Why are the people of the West selecting one sort of myrtle [as against some other sort]?"

[C]   [He was answered:] Now has he not heard that which R. Simon said in the name of R. Joshua b. Levi, "'And that they should publish and proclaim in all their towns and in Jerusalem, Go out to the hills and bring branches of olive, wild olive, myrtle, palm, and other leafy trees to make booths, as it is written' (Neh. 8:15). [This indicates that there are types of myrtle that are used for the *sukkah*, and there are other types that are used in the *lulab*.]"

[D]   Is not a myrtle branch identical to a leafy branch?

[E]   There is a kind of myrtle for the *sukkah,* and a kind of leafy branch for the *lulab.* [So it is quite appropriate to select a kind of myrtle suitable for the *lulab,* as distinct from the kind suitable for use in the *sukkah.*]

[F]   R. Zeira [when he heard this teaching] made a point [of memorizing it].

[**III.A**]   He who prepares a *lulab* for his own use says, "Blessed . . . who has sanctified us by his commandments, and commanded us to make a *lulab.*"

[B]   If he did so for someone else, he says, ". . . to make a *lulab* for His Name."

[C]   When he takes it, what does he say?

[D]   "Blessed . . . who has sanctified us by his commandments and commanded us concerning taking up the *lulab.*"

[E]   And he prays over it, saying, "Blessed . . . who has kept us alive and sustained us and brought us to this season."

[F]   And he says a blessing over it every time that he takes it up.

[G]   How do they say a blessing over the Hanukkah light?

[H]   Rab said, "Blessed . . . who has sanctified us by his commandments and commanded us concerning the commandment to kindle the Hanukkah light."

[I]   All concur that on the occasion of the first day of the Festival, one says, ". . . concerning the taking of the *lulab.*"

[J]   Where there is a dispute, it concerns the other days of the festival.

[K]   R. Yohanan said, "[One says,] '. . . concerning taking up the *lulab.*'"

[L]   And R. Joshua b. Levi said, "[One says,] '. . . concerning the commandments of the elders [by whose authority we take up the *lulab*].'" [But it is not by the command of the Torah, on the remainder of the days of the festival. The Torah's commandment pertains solely to the first day of the festival.]

[M]   What did Rab say concerning the *lulab?*

[N]   Now if with regard to the festival of Hanukkah, which derives solely from the authority of the scribes, he maintains that one says, "Concerning the commandment of lighting the Hanukkah light," with respect to the *lulab*, which, to begin with, derives from the Torah, is it not an argument *a fortiori* [that one should say the blessing as Yohanan maintains]?

[O]   What did R. Joshua b. Levi say with regard to the case of Hanukkah?

[P]   Now if in the matter of the *lulab*, which derives from the authority of the Torah, one says, ". . . concerning the commandment of the elders," Hanukkah, which is a matter of scribal authority to begin with, all the more so [one should say that the commandment derives merely from the elders].

[Q]   The sole point at which we must raise a question, then, is what R. Yohanan said with regard to Hanukkah.

[IV.A] Hiyya son of Rab said a blessing for each time [one takes the *lulab*].

[B]   R. Hunah said a blessing only one time alone.

[C]   R. Huna in the name of R. Joseph: "The reasoning of R. Hunah is this:

[D]   "Separating tithe from doubtfully tithed produce derives from the authority of the scribes, and taking up the *lulab* on the other days of the Festival, after the first, likewise derives from the authority of the scribes.

[E]   "Just as in the case of separating tithe from doubtfully tithed produce, one does not say a blessing, so with regard to taking up the *lulab* on the other days of the Festival, one does not say a blessing on that account."

Unit I provides an exegetical basis and clarification for Ishmael's position, M. 3:4A–B. The remainder of the Talmud goes off in its own direction. Unit II indicates that one must choose the right kind of species for the stated purpose. Unit III takes up the question of what blessing is to be said over the *lulab*, and whether the blessing is to be said through the Festival or only on the first day, of which Scripture speaks. Unit IV pursues this same question.

3:5

[A]   *A stolen or dried up citron is invalid.*

[B]   *And one deriving from an asherah or from an apostate town is invalid.*

[C]   *[If it derived from] orlah-fruit, it is invalid.*

[D]   *[If it derived from] unclean heave-offering, it is invalid.*

[E]   *[If it derived from] clean heave-offering, one should not carry it. But if he carried it, it is valid.*

[F]   *One which is in the status of doubtfully tithed produce—*

[G]   *the House of Shammai declare invalid.*

[H]   *And the House of Hillel declare valid.*

[I]   *And one in the status of second tithe in Jerusalem one should not carry. But if he carried it, it is valid.*

[I.A]   It is written, "The fruit of a goodly tree" (Lev. 23:40).

[B]   This refers to a tree the fruit of which is good, and the wood of which also is good.

[C]   And what sort of tree is that? It is the *etrog*.

[D]   If you say that it refers to a pomegranate, its fruit is good but its wood is not good.

[E]   If you say that it refers to a carob, its wood is good, but its fruit is not good.

[F]   [What then meets both qualifications?] It is the *etrog*.

[G]   What is the meaning of *hadar* [goodly]?

[H]   Said R. Levi, "That [the fruit] remains [*dar*] in the tree from year to year."

[I]   Said R. Tanhuma, "Aqilas translated, '*Hadar*' [goodly] as '*Hydor*' [the Greek word for water]. It then refers to a tree that grows by water."

[J]   R. Simeon b. Yohai taught, "And you shall take for yourself the fruit of a goodly tree" (Lev. 23:40). This refers to one the fruit of which is good, and the wood of which is good.

[K]   The flavor of the fruit is to be the same as the flavor of the wood, and the flavor of the wood is to be the same as the flavor of the fruit.

[L]   Its fruit, moreover, resembles its wood, and its wood resembles its fruit.

[M]   And what is this? It is the *etrog.*

[II.A]   R. Jacob, the Southerner, raised the question [concerning M. Er. 3:2]: "The Mishnah [at M. Er. 3:2] does not accord with the view of the House of Shammai.

[B]   "For we have learned: *As to an* etrog *deriving from doubtfully tithed produce the House of Shammai declare invalid, and the House of Hillel declare valid. And one in the status of second tithe in Jerusalem one should not carry, but if he carried it, it is valid [M. 3:5F–I]."*

The citron must be available for eating, and, it follows, what may not be eaten, M. 3:5C, D, also will not serve. Doubtfully tithed produce must be properly tithed; since, when taken up, they may not be eaten because they require further preparation, the House of Shammai invalidate them. Since they nonetheless can be made suitable for eating, the House of Hillel validate them. Second tithe in Jerusalem may be eaten, but falls under the rule of E. Unit **I** supplies M. with various scriptural foundations, and unit **II** is primary to M. Er. 3:2. It does not belong here at all, but is inserted because of the occurrence of the present passage of the Mishnah.

3:6

[A]   *[If] scars covered the greater part of it,*

[B]   *[if] its nipple was removed,*

[C]   *[if] it was peeled, split, had a hole and so lacked any part whatsoever, it is invalid.*

[D]   *[If] scars covered the lesser part of it,*

[E]   *[if] its stalk was removed,*

[F]   *[if] it had a hole but lacked no part whatsoever,*

[G]   it is valid.

[H]   *A dark-colored citron is invalid.*

[I]   *And one which is green like a leek—*

[J]   *R. Meir declares it valid.*

[K]   *And R. Judah declares it invalid.*

[I.A]   R. Isaac bar Nahman in the name of Samuel: "All those traits that invalidate do so only on the first day of the Festival alone."

[II.A]   There they say, "[Even if it is scarred] on the greater part of it only on one side [it is invalid].

[B]   "[If] its nipple [was scarred (PM)], it is as if the greater part of it [was scarred]."

[III.A]   *If its nipple was removed [M. 3:6B]:*

[B]   There they say, "Its rose."

[C]   R. Isaac bar Haqola said, "The spindle."

[IV.A]   *If it was split [M. 3:6B]:*

[B]   But it did not perforate within [through the skin], it remains valid.

[C]   This is in line with that which we have learned there: *If its stalk was removed, if it had a hole but lacked no part whatsoever, it is valid [M. 3:6E–G].*

[V.A]   A dark-colored citron is invalid [M. 3:6H]:

[B]   That which comes from Ethiopia is valid [vis-à-vis M. 3:6H].

[C]   *One which is green like a leek [M. 3:6I]:*

[D]   R. Zeira asked before R. Imi, "Is it exactly as green as a leek, or is it merely similar to leek-green?"

[E]   He said to him, "Exactly as green as a leek."

[F]   *What is the greenest of the green shades? R. Eliezer says, "Like wax and like a green gourd." Sumkhos says, "Like the wing of a peacock and like the branches of a palm tree."*

[G]   *What is the reddest of the red? Like the finest crimson which is in the sea [T. Neg. 1:5B–F].*

[H]   And here the law has said this? [With reference to leek, how can it be regarded as a deep green?]

[I]   Said R. Phineas, "The case there [with respect to the leprosy-sign of garments and skins] is different, for Scripture speaks of pale green [so leeks would not belong at F]."

The Talmud's several units systematically work through and complement M.'s clauses, defining terms, revising readings, and otherwise clarifying the rules.

3:7 (L + V: 3:7–8)

[A]   *The measure of the smallest [acceptable] citron—*

[B]   *R. Meir says, "The size of a nut."*

[C]   *R. Judah says, "The size of an egg."*

[D]   *And as to the largest [acceptable size]—*

[E]   *"It must be of such a size that one can hold two in one hand," the words of R. Judah.*

[F]   *R. Yose says, "Even one in two hands."*

[I.A]   An *etrog* that was half-ripe—

[B]   R. Aqiba says, "It is not regarded as fruit."

[C]   And sages say, "It is fruit."

[D]   R. Ila, R. Yose in the name of R. Eleazar: "The view of R. Simeon accords with the thesis of R. Aqiba, his teacher.

[E]   "Just as R. Aqiba has said, 'A half-ripe *etrog* is not fruit,' so R. Simeon has said, 'A half-ripe *etrog* is not fruit.'"

[F]   [Assuming Aqiba's meaning is that the half-ripe *etrog* in no way is regarded as fruit, hence is exempt from tithing,] said R. Yose, "And is it the case that whatever is valid for use as part of a *lulab* is liable for tithes, while whatever is not suitable for use as part of a *lulab* is not liable for tithes?"

[G]   They objected, "Lo, there is the case of the *etrog* that is spotted, lo, there is the case of an *etrog* grown in a frame, lo, there is the case of an *etrog* in the shape of a round ball. Lo, these are invalid for use in a *lulab,* but liable for tithing."

[H]   [Since it is assumed that Simeon regards these as not liable, while Aqiba holds that they are,] it stands to reason that R. Simeon will concur with R. Aqiba [that they are invalid for use as part of a *lulab*], while R. Aqiba will not concur with R. Simeon [that they also are exempt from tithing].

[I]   R. Simeon will concur with R. Aqiba, since Scripture refers to fruit, while these are not fruit.

[J]   R. Aqiba will not concur with R. Simeon, since this is the fact: "Lo, if it is an *etrog* that is spotted, lo, it if it is an *etrog* grown in a frame, lo, if it is an *etrog* in the shape of a round ball, these are invalid for use in a *lulab,* but liable for tithing."

[II.A]   [With regard to M. 3:7B, *the size of a nut:*] We have learned to repeat the formulation of the Mishnah, "Like a nut."

[B]   There is a Tanna who teaches, "Up to the size of a nut."

[C]   The one who has said, "Like the size of a nut," accepts one that is as big as a nut.

[D]   The one who has said, "Up to the size of a nut," will declare invalid one that is as big as a nut.

[III.A]   [With reference to M. 3:7D–F,] said R. Yose, "If Scripture had said, 'And the tops of palm branches,' it would have been well [for Judah's view that one can hold two in one hand].

[B]   "But Scripture has said only, 'The tops of palm branches.'

[C]   "That is, even if this one is in one hand, and that one is in the other hand."

[D]   They said concerning R. Aqiba that he came into the synagogue bearing an *etrog* on his shoulders.

Unit **I** carries forward the definition of the suitable *etrog* and so serves M. 3:5–6 rather than the present unit. But the issue is separate and secondary in any case. Units **II** and **III** clarify minor points of M.

3:8 (L + V: 3:9–10)

[A] *"They bind up the* lulab *[palm branch, willow branch, and myrtle branch] only with [strands of] its own species," the words of R. Judah.*

[B] *R. Meir says, "Even with a rope [it is permitted to bind up the* lulab*]."*

[C] *Said R. Meir, "M^cSH B: The townsfolk of Jerusalem bound up their palm branches with gold threads."*

[D] *They said to him, "But underneath they [in fact had] tied it up with [strands of] its own species."*

[E] *And at what point [in the* Hallel *psalms, 113–118] did they shake [the* lulab*]?*

[F] *"At 'O give thanks unto the Lord' (Ps. 118), beginning and end; and at, 'Save now, we beseech thee, O Lord'" (Ps. 118:25), the words of the House of Hillel.*

[G] *And the House of Shammai say, "Also: At, 'O Lord, we beseech thee, send now prosperity'" (Ps. 118:25).*

[H] *Said R. Aqiba, "I was watching Rabban Gamaliel and R. Joshua, for all the people waved their palm branches, but they waved their palm branches only at, 'Save now, we beseech thee, O Lord'" (Ps. 118:25).*

[I] *He who was on a trip and had no* lulab *to carry—*

[J] *when he reaches home, should carry the* lulab *at his own table.*

[K] *[If] he did not carry his* lulab *in the morning, he should carry it at dusk,*

[L] *for the entire day is a suitable time for the palm branch.*

[I.A] [With reference to M. 3:8E–H:] Lo, in "O give thanks to the Lord, for he is good" (Ps. 118:1), do they not [wave the *lulab*, in line with M. 3:8H]?

[B]   [His intent was] to exclude [waving at] "O Lord, we beseech thee, send now prosperity" (Ps. 118:25). [The purpose, M. 3:8H, was to reject the position of the House of Shammai at M. 3:8G.]

[II.A]   [With reference to M. 3:8/I–L] R. Hiyya bar Ashi in the name of Rab: "This one who gets up very early to go on a trip takes the *lulab* and shakes it, the ram's horn and sounds it [before he leaves home]. When, later in the day, the time for saying the *Shema* comes, lo, this one recites the *Shema* and says the Prayer."

[III.A]   It has been taught: One has to shake the *lulab* three times.

[B]   R. Zeira asked, "Does a shake in one direction count as one, and a shake in another direction count as one, or is it an up and then a down motion in one direction that counts as one shake?

[C]   There we have learned: *The stain [of blood] must be scoured with each of them three times [M. Nid. 9:7].*

[D]   R. Zeira asked, "Does a scouring in one direction represent one, a scouring in the other, a second, or is it an up and then a down motion in one direction that counts as one scouring?"

Unit **I** clarifies M. 3:8H's information. Unit **II** supplements M. 3:8/I. Unit **III** carries forward the interest of unit **II**.

3:9 (L + V: 3:11)

[A]   *He for whom a slave, woman, or minor read answers after them by saying what they say.*

[B]   *But it is a curse to him.*

[C]   *If an adult male read for him, he answers after him [only] "Halleluyah."*

[I.A]   It has been taught: But they have said, "A woman says a blessing for her husband, a slave for his master, a child for his father."

[B]   There is no problem in understanding why a woman may say a blessing for her husband, a slave for his master.

[C]   But as to a minor for his father, did not R. Aha say in the name of R. Yose b. Nehorai, "'Whatever they have said in respect to a

minor['s doing a religious deed] is in order to educate him'?
[Since the child is not subject to the religious duty, if he says a
blessing, how can he serve to say it in behalf of his father, who is
subject to the religious duty?]"

[D]   Interpret the rule to speak of a case in which the father answers
"Amen" after him.

[E]   That is in line with what we have learned there: *He for whom a
slave, woman, or minor read [the Hallel] answers after them by
saying what they say. But it is a curse to him [M. 3:9A–B].*

[F]   They have further said, "May a curse come upon one twenty years
old he needs [the help of the reading of someone] ten years old."

The Talmud is primary to Y. Ber. 3:3, Y. R.H. 3:10.

3:10 (L + V: 3:12)

[A]   *Where they are accustomed to repeat [the last nine verses of
Ps. 118], let one repeat.*

[B]   *[Where it is the custom] to say them only once, let one say them
only once.*

[C]   *[Where it is the custom] to say a blessing after it, let one say a
blessing after it.*

[D]   *Everything follows the custom of the locality.*

[E]   *He who buys a lulab [palm branch, myrtle branch, willow
branch] from his fellow in the Seventh Year—[the seller] gives
him a citron as a gift.*

[F]   *For one is not permitted to buy [the citron] in the Seventh Year.*

[I.A] Rab and Samuel: One said, "It is Halleluyah [in one word],"
and the other said, "It is Hallelu Yah [in two words]."

[B]   He who says that it is two words maintains that the word may be
divided, but it may not be erased [since the word for God, Yah,
is consecrated].

[C]   He who says that it is Halleluyah [in one word] permits the word
to be blotted out [since the Yah is not written as the name of
God] but does not allow it to be divided into two.

[D]   Now we do not know who has taken this position, and who has stated that one.

[E]   On the basis on what Rab has said, "I heard from my uncle [Hiyya], 'If someone were to give me the Book of Psalms written by R. Meir, I should be prepared to blot out every appearance of the word, Halleluyah, in it, for he did not write the word intending to sanctify [the word for God when he wrote the word, Halleluyah],' it follows that he is the one who said, 'It is Halleluyah [as one word].'"

[F]   [54a] A statement of rabbis differs [from this view of Rab's]. For R. Simeon said in the name of R. Joshua b. Levi, "The book of Psalms makes use of ten different expressions of praise [for God]: Fortunate, victory, melody, song, psalm, instruction, joy, thanksgiving, prayer, blessing.

[G]   "The greatest of all is Halleluyah, because it encompasses the divine Name and praise simultaneously. [Hence, Yah, in the word Halleluyah, stands for the divine Name.]"

[II.A]   R. Zeira asked before R. Abbahu, "What do we answer after the one who recites the *Hallel* psalms?"

[B]   R. Abba of Kipa before R. Jonah, "Answer thus and so [as Scripture specifies]."

[C]   R. Eleazar did not respond thus and so.

[D]   Rab in the name of R. Abba bar Hanah in the name of Rab: "And that rule [as to replying] applies to him who responded by reciting the opening sentence of each paragraph."

[E]   R. Zeira asked, "And what are these opening sentences?"

[F]   "Praise the Lord! Praise, O servants of the Lord, praise the name of the Lord! Blessed be the name of the Lord from this time forth and for evermore!" (Ps. 113:1–2).

[III.A]   [With reference to M. 3:10B–C,] they asked before R. Hiyya bar Ba, "How do we know that if one heard the *Hallel* psalms but did not respond, he nonetheless has carried out his obligation?"

[B]   He said to him, "It is on the basis of the fact that we see our great rabbis standing in the congregation, and these say, 'Blessed is he . . . ,' and they reply, 'Who comes in the name of the Lord,' and both these and those thereby carry out their obligation."

[**IV.**A]   R. Hoshaiah taught, "A man answers, 'Amen,' [to others who say Grace], even though he did not eat.

[B]   "But he does not say, 'Blessed is He, of whose food we have eaten,' if he did not eat."

[**V.**A]   It has been taught: They do not say an "orphan-Amen," or a "cut-off Amen."

[B]   What is an "orphan-Amen"?

[C]   Said R. Hunah, "It is one in which a person is liable to say a blessing, and he answers, 'Amen,' but he does not know on what account."

[**VI.**A]   It has been taught: As to a pagan who said a blessing for the Name—they answer, "Amen," after him.

[B]   If he said a blessing using the Name, they do not answer, "Amen," after him.

[C]   Said R. Tanhuma, "If an idolater blesses you, answer after him, 'Amen.'

[D]   "For it is written, 'You shall be blessed above all peoples; there shall not be male or female barren among you, or among your cattle'" (Deut. 7 : 14).

[E]   An idolater met R. Ishmael and blessed him. He said to him, "The proper reply for what you have said already has been stated." Another met him and cursed him.

[F]   He said to him, "The proper reply for what you have said already has been stated."

[G]   His disciples said to him, "Rabbi, how is it possible that you said to this one precisely what you said to the other?"

[H]   He said to them, "And has it not been written, 'Cursed be every one who curses you, and blessed be every one who blesses you!'" (Gen. 27 : 29)?

[**VII.**A]   [With reference to M. 3 : 10A–B,] Rabbi would repeat certain words in it.

[B]   R. Eleazar b. Parta would augment certain words in it.

[**VIII.**A]   [With reference to M. 3 : 10E–F,] said R. Eleazar, "This rule represents the view of the Elders of the Galilee.

[B]   "For the Elders of the Galilee say, 'It is forbidden to hand over
to someone suspect of not observing the taboos of the Seventh
Year [money sufficient for] food for two meals [since he is assumed to use the money to purchase food grown in the Sab-
batical Year, and one may not do so].' [Hence the *etrog* must
come as a gift.]"

[C]   Said R. Mattenayyah, "Interpret the rule to represent the view
of all parties. It refers to a time in which *etrog*s were sold at high
prices [and proceeds received for the *etrog*s by themselves would
be sufficient to purchase two meals]. [Hence under these circumstances all parties maintain the same view.]"

[D]   There is the following case: *Etrog*s were in short supply there [in
Babylonia], and R. Nahman b. Jacob gave an *etrog* as a gift to his
son.

[E]   He said to him, "When you have taken possession of it and of
the religious duty to be done with it, return it to me."

With regard to M. 3:10E–F, in the Seventh Year one may not
purchase produce grown in that year. The citron, picked that
year, alone falls under the rule. Hence the citron is to be given
as a gift, while the other items may be bought and sold. The
other items are not food but wood and may be bought and sold.
Unit **I** is primary at Y. Meg. 1:9. It is included here because
of the allusion to the *Hallel* psalms, which use the word, Halleluyah. The entire set, **I–VI**, appears together at Y. Meg. 1:9.
But units **II** and **III** directly address M. 3:10C, what blessing or
other response is said after reciting the *Hallel* psalms. Hence
the framer of the whole moved everything together to this point
because of units **II** and **III,** and used the entire lot together at
Y. Meg. 1:9 because of unit **I.** Units **VII** and **VIII** amplify the
specified elements of M.

3:11 (L + V: 3:13–14)

[A]   *At first the* lulab *was carried in the Temple for seven days, and
in the provinces, for one day.*

[B]   *When the Temple was destroyed, Rabban Yohanan b. Zakkai
ordained that the* lulab *should be carried in the provinces
seven days,*

[C]   *as a memorial to the Temple;*

[D]   *and that the whole of the day on which the* omer *is waved should be forbidden [for the use of new produce, which may be used only from the waving of the* omer *and thereafter; this had formerly been offered at noon].*

[E]   *[If] the first festival day of the Festival [of Sukkot] coincides with the Sabbath, all the people bring their* lulabs *to the synagogue [on the day before].*

[F]   *On the next day they get up and come along. Each one finds his own and takes it.*

[G]   *For sages have said, "A person does not fulfill his obligation [to wave the* lulab*] on the first day of the Festival by using the* lulab *of his fellow.*

[H]   *"And on all other days of the Festival, one does fulfill his obligation [to wave the* lulab*] by using the* lulab *of his fellow."*

[I]   *R. Yose says, "[If] the first day of the Festival [of Sukkot] coincides with the Sabbath, [if] one forgot and brought his* lulab *out into the public domain, he is exempt [from the obligation to bring a sin-offering],*

[J]   *"because he brought it out [intending to do what is] permitted."*

[I.A]   It is written, "You shall rejoice before the Lord your God seven days" (Lev. 23:40).

[B]   There is a Tanna who teaches, "It is with regard to the rejoicing with the *lulab* that Scripture speaks."

[C]   There is a Tanna who teaches, "It is with regard to the rejoicing [brought on by eating the meat] of peace-offerings that the Scripture speaks."

[D]   [The written text: He who has said that it is with regard to the rejoicing of the peace-offerings that Scripture speaks maintains that doing so on the first day is based on the authority of the Torah, and doing so on the other days is on the authority of the Torah as well. PM's corrected text:] He who says that it is with regard to the rejoicing with the *lulab* that Scripture speaks holds that doing so on the first day is based on the authority of the Torah, and doing so on the other days also is based on the authority of the Torah.

[E]   Consequently, in making his ordinance [M. 3:11, transferring to the provinces the rite of the Temple of carrying the *lulab* all

seven days, doing in the synagogue what was done in the Temple],
R. Yohanan ben Zakkai made his ordinance relying upon the law
of the Torah.

[F]   [The written text: But he who has said that it is with regard to
the rejoicing with the *lulab* that the Scripture spoke for the first
day, as a matter of Torah law, but for the other days as a matter
of law based on the authority of the scribes, then Rabban Yohanan
ben Zakkai made his decree resting on the authority of the scribes
(as well). PM's corrected text:] But he who says that it is with
the rejoicing of the peace-offerings that Scripture speaks maintains that doing so on the first day is a matter of Torah law, but
for the other days it is a matter of law based on the authority of
the scribes, then Rabban Yohanan ben Zakkai made his decree
resting on the authority of scribes [as well]. [Now the carrying
of the *lulab* all seven days in the Temple was an ordinance of
scribes, and doing so in the provinces, after the destruction, was
an ordinance based on the authority of scribes tacked on to an
ordinance based on the authority of scribes.]

[G]   Now is it possible that there should be one ordinance tacked on
to another such ordinance? [This question is not answered.]

[II.A]   [As to the view that taking the *lulab* does not override the restrictions of the Sabbath except when the first day of the Festival
coincides with the Sabbath, even in the Temple, which is implied at M. 3:11E and made explicit at M. 4:1,] associates asked
before R. Jonah, "Just as you say, 'Seven days you shall present
offerings by fire to the Lord; on the eighth day you shall hold
a holy convocation and present an offering by fire to the Lord;
it is a solemn assembly; you shall do no laborious work' (Lev.
23:36), and there is no week of seven days without a Sabbath
[indicating that one carries out the festivals' additional-offerings
when the Sabbath coincides with a festival],

[B]   "so, along these same lines, 'And you shall take for yourself on
the first day the fruit of goodly trees, branches of palm trees,
and boughs of leafy trees, and willows of the brook; and you
shall rejoice before the Lord your God seven days' (Lev. 23:40).
Here too it is specified that there are seven days of celebration,
and there is no week of seven days without a Sabbath. [Accord-
ingly, even when the first day of the Festival does not coincide
with the Sabbath, on the Sabbath taking the *lulab* should be
permitted, since the clear implication of Scripture is that that
should be done.]"

[C]   He said to them, "This case is different, for it is said, 'And you shall take for yourself on the first day . . .' (Lev. 23:40). The Scripture has thus distinguished the first day from the others. [What applies that first day is then different.]"

[D]   If that is the case, then in the sanctuary let the taking of the *lulab* on the first day that coincides with the Sabbath override the restrictions of the Sabbath. But in the provinces, let it *not* do so [as against M. 3:11E]!

[E]   Said R. Jonah, "If it were written, 'And you shall take . . . *before the Lord your God*' [that is, this additional language indicates that the taking is to be before the Lord, hence in the Temple], I should say, Here you have an exclusionary clause [excluding taking the *lulab* all seven days, inclusive of the Sabbath, in the provinces]. In another place, you have an inclusionary phrase [indicating the opposite]. But it says, 'You will take for yourself . . . ,' indicating, it is under all circumstances.

[F]   "'And you will rejoice before the Lord your God for seven days' indicates that it is Jerusalem. [Thus there are grounds for both the rule that the *lulab*-rite overrides the Sabbath in the Temple, even when the first day of the Festival does not fall on the Sabbath, and the rule that in the provinces the *lulab*-rite overrides the Sabbath *only* when the first day of the Festival coincides with the Sabbath.]"

[III.A]   [With reference to M. 3:11/I–J:] Associates say, "The reason for the position of R. Yose is that a positive commandment [to carry the *lulab*] overrides the negative commandment [of not carrying an object from private to public domain on the Sabbath]."

[B]   Said to them R. Yose, "That is not the consideration important to R. Yose [of M. 3:11/I–J]. Rather, it was on the basis of the reason behind what R. Ila said. And so has it been taught there:

[C]   "This was the custom in Jerusalem. A man would go to the synagogue, with his *lulab* in his hand. He would recite the *Shema* and say the Prayer with his *lulab* in his hand.

[D]   [What follows is in T.'s amplified version: **"He would arise to read the translation (of the Scripture) or to take his place before the ark, with his *lulab* in his hand.**

[E]   **"(If) he arose to read in the Torah or to raise his hands (in the priestly benediction of the congregation), he would put it down on the ground.**

[F]   "When he went out of the synagogue, his *lulab* was in his hand.

[G]   "When he went in to visit the sick and to comfort mourners, his *lulab* was in his hand.

[H]   "But when he entered the study-house, he would give it to his son or his messenger and return it to his house" (**T. Suk. 2:10**).] [The point is that it was customary to carry the *lulab* out of devotion to that religious duty.]

[I]   Once one has put down the *lulab* [having performed his religious duty with it], it is forbidden to carry it about, [since there is no further religious requirement involved].

[J]   Said R. Abun, "That is to say that it is forbidden to derive benefit [from the *lulab*, except for a religious purpose]."

[K]   It has been taught: They carry aromatic spices on the Sabbath to a sick person for use as a scent.

[L]   Rabbis of Caesarea say, "As to a willow, it is permitted to wave it for a sick person on the Sabbath."

[M]   Is the same rule [as Yose gives at M. 3:11/I–J] so for the knife for performing a circumcision, is the same so for unleavened bread?

[N]   On the basis of what R. Yohanan has said, "In the view of R. Yose, even if one has completed the rite of circumcision and left, he may go back [carrying the knife] on account of the sherds [of flesh that must be clipped off,] though these do not invalidate the fundamental rite of circumcision,"

[O]   it follows that the same rule [as is given at M. 3:1/I–J] applies [in Yose's view] to the knife for performing the rite of circumcision and to the bringing of unleavened bread.

The ordinances take account of the destruction of the Temple. The *omer*, M. 3:11D, was offered on the fifteenth of Nisan, so from the afternoon onward, it had been permitted to eat produce harvested in the present growing cycle. But Yohanan prohibited use of the new produce for the whole of the fifteenth of Nisan, as a memorial to the Temple. Taking the *lulab* all seven days, M. 3:11B, means that the prohibitions of the Sabbath must now be introduced, M. 3:11E–J. Taking the *lulab* on the first day of the festival coinciding with the Sabbath overrides the restrictions of the Sabbath (a concept made explicit at M. 4 : 2). We now provide for that contingency. There is no need to carry the *lulab* to the synagogue; it is left there overnight, since one must do beforehand what can be done in advance. Unit **I** carries forward the analysis of Yohanan ben Zakkai's ordinance, M. 3 : 11A–C, and its basis in legal theory. Unit **II** asks about the Scriptural foundations of M. 3 : 11E, that is, the matter of the relationship of the Sabbath to taking the *lulab*, specifically, whether one may do so if the first day of the Festival does not coincide with the Sabbath. Here too the Scriptural rules are subjected to exegesis so that the basis for M.'s rules and implied rules is indicated. Unit **III** brings us to M. 3 : 11/I–J. Yose's reasoning is explained within two theories, the first, **III.A**, rejected, the second, **III.Bff.**, confirmed. The latter is simply that a person is taken up with doing the religious duty regarding the *lulab*, and, consequently, is forgiven for his lapse of attention.

3:12 (L + V: 3:15)

[A]   *A woman receives the* lulab *from her son or husband and puts it back into water on the Sabbath.*

[B]   *R. Judah says, "On the Sabbath they put it back into [the same water], on the festival day they add water, and on the intermediate days of the festival they change the water."*

[C]   *A minor who knows how to wave the* lulab *is liable to the requirement of waving the* lulab.

[I.A]   [If a minor] knows how to wave the *lulab*, he is liable to the requirement of waving the *lulab*.

[B]   If he knows how to wrap himself up in a cloak, he is liable to put show-fringes on his garment.

[C]   If he knows how to speak, his father teaches him the language of Torah.

[D]   If he knows how to watch out for his hands, people may eat food in the status of heave-offering relying on his hands [if he touched it].

[E]   [If he knows how to keep] his body, they eat food prepared in conditions of cultic cleanness relying on his person [if the food touched it].

[F]   But he does not go before the ark [to lead the congregation in prayer], raise up his hands, or stand on the platform [as a Levitical singer], until his beard has filled out.

[G]   Rabbi says, "And one does them all at the age of twenty and onward, as it is said, 'They appointed the Levites, from twenty years old and upward, to have the oversight of the work of the house of the Lord'" (Ezra 3:8).

The woman handles the *lulab* on the Sabbath, even though she is not obligated to wave it. This triggers the addition of B and C, two further rules relevant to M. 3:12A, first, on changing the water, second, on who else is obligated to take up the *lulab*. The Talmud complements M. 3:12C.

4 Yerushalmi Sukkah Chapter Four

4:1

[A]   [54b] *[The rites of]* the lulab *and the willow branch [carried by the priests around the altar, M. 4:3] are for six or seven [days].*

[B]   *The recitation of the Hallel psalms and the rejoicing are for eight [days].*

[C]   *[The requirement of dwelling in the]* sukkah *and the water libation are for seven days.*

[D]   *And the flute playing is for five or six.*

[E]   *The* lulab *is for seven days: How so?*

[F]   *[If] the first festival day of the Festival coincided with the Sabbath, the* lulab *is for seven days.*

[G]   *But [if it coincided] with any other day, it is for six days.*

[H]   *The willow-branch [rite] is for seven days: How so?*

[I]   *[If] the seventh day of the willow branch coincided with the Sabbath, the willow-branch [rite] is for seven days.*

[J]   *But [if it coincided] with any other day, it is for six days.*

[I.A]   R. Zeirah, R. Ila, R. Yose in the name of R. Yohanan: "The willow-branch rite was revealed to Moses at Sinai [orally, not in writing]."

[B]   That view does not accord with the position of Abba Saul. For **Abba Saul says, "The rite of the willow branch derives from the teaching of the Torah.**

[C]   "'Willows of the brook' (Lev. 23:40) in the plural speaks of two matters, a willow for the *lulab,* and a willow for the Temple [rite]" [T. Suk. 3:1/I].

[D]   R. Ba, R. Hiyya in the name of R. Yohanan: "The willow and the water libation were revealed to Moses at Sinai [with no basis in the written Torah]."

[E]   That is not in accord with the view of R. Aqiba.

[F]   For R. Aqiba said, "The water libation derives from the teaching of the Torah.

[G]   "[Citing Num. 29:19:] 'On the second day . . . and their drink-offerings' [in the plural, as against Num. 29:16, '. . . and its drink-offering,' so too for Num. 29:22, for the third day; Num. 29:25, for the fourth day, Num. 29:28, for the fifth day. Then: Num. 29:31:] 'On the sixth day . . . and its drink-offerings.' [And also, Num. 29:33:] 'On the seventh day . . . according to the ordinance.' We have, then, reference to an M, Y, M, spelling out the Hebrew word for water, so indicating that there is a libation-offering of water."

[II.A]   [With reference to M. Sheb. 1:6, served by the foregoing, it is permitted to plough a field planted with saplings up to the New Year of the Seventh Year, but forbidden to plough a field planted with old trees beginning in the spring prior to the Seventh Year. This is claimed to represent a law revealed to Moses at Sinai. At M. Sheb. 1:6 it is stated, *If ten saplings are spread out over a seah's space, the whole space may be ploughed for their sake until the New Year.*] R. Hiyya bar Ba asked before R. Yohanan, "Why at this time, then, do they plough among old trees?"

[B]   He said to him, "When the law was revealed, it was given with the stipulation that if they wanted to plough they might do so."

[C]   R. Ba bar Zabeda in the name of R. Honayya of Beth Hauran: "The willow-rite, the water-libation, and the rule of ten saplings [of M. Sheb. 1:6] are based on the foundations of the prophets."

[D]   Does he differ [from Yohanan, who maintains that it was a law revealed to Moses at Sinai]?

[E]   R. Yose b. R. Bun in the name of Levi: "Thus was the law as they originally had it in hand, but they forgot it, and the second group went and made the law conform to the original opinion of the former one.

[F]   "This serves to teach you that any matter for which a court is prepared to give its life will in the end endure as if it had been revealed to Moses at Sinai."

[G]   This conforms to that which R. Mana said, " 'For it is no trifle for you, [but it is your life, and thereby you shall live long in the land which you are going over the Jordan to possess]' (Deut. 32:47).

[H]   "If it is a trifle, it is on your account.

[I]   "Why? Because you do not work hard at it.

[J]   " 'But it is your life' (Deut. 32:47).

[K]   "When is it your life? When you work hard at it."

[III.A] R. Yohanan said to R. Hiyya bar Ba, "O Babylonian! Two matters came up in your possession [from the Exile], prostration on a fast day [by spreading out the hands and feet], and the willow-rite on the seventh day [M. 4:1A, H–I]."

[B]   Rabbis of Caesarea say, "Also the matter of blood-letting [indicating the times at which it is, or is not, beneficial]."

[C]   R. Simeon instructed those who calculate the calendar, "Pay attention that you do not so arrange matters that there is a requirement to sound the ram's horn on the Sabbath [that is, so that the New Year not coincide with the Sabbath] and also so that there is no willow-rite on the Sabbath. [These rites do not override the prohibitions of the Sabbath.]

[D]   "But if you are forced to do so, have the sounding of the ram's horn on the Sabbath, and do not have the willow-rite on the Sabbath."

M. 4:1E–G and H–J explain why M. 4:1A's items may be done either on six or on seven days. Only if the first festival day of the Festival coincides with the Sabbath are these rites carried out on the Sabbath. If the first festival day of the Festival is on any other day, then for the Sabbath which falls in the intermediate days of the festival these rites are suspended (compare M. 3:12).

That is the point repeated at E–G and H–J. It will not be relevant to M. 4:1B or C, since there is no problem with the Sabbath for these rites, or to M. 4:1D, because there is no basis for permitting the flute playing to override the restrictions of the Sabbath in any event. Unit **I** takes up the origin of the willow-branch rite, showing that it derives from an oral law revealed to Moses at Sinai. This discussion, which also serves Y. Sheb. 1:5, carries in its wake unit **II,** primary to that discussion and hardly in place here. But **II.**C shows the pertinence of the whole. Unit **III** is pertinent to M. 4:1A for obvious reasons.

4:2

[A]   *The religious requirement of the lulab [on the Sabbath]: How so?*

[B]   *[If] the first festival day of the Festival coincided with the Sabbath, they bring their lulabs to the Temple mount.*

[C]   *And the attendants take them from them and arrange them on the roof of the portico.*

[D]   *But old people leave theirs in a special room.*

[E]   *They teach them to make the following statement: "To whomever my lulab comes, lo, it is given to him as a gift."*

[F]   *On the next day they get up and come along.*

[G]   *And the attendants toss them before them.*

[H]   *They grab at lulabs and hit one another.*

[I]   *Now when the court saw that this was leading to a dangerous situation, they ordained that each and every one should take his lulab in his own home.*

[I.A]   R. Jacob, the Southerner, raised the question: "The Mishnah-passage [M. 4:2E] before us does not conform to the view of R. Dosa.

[B]   **"For R. Dosa said, '[In declaring produce available to the poor as ownerless property,] in the morning a person has to declare, "Whatever the poor will collect today among the sheaves as ownerless property, lo, this is ownerless property." [This must be said in advance.]'**

[C]   "R. Judah says, 'This may be said in the evening [even after the property has changed hands].'

[D]   "And sages say, 'What is declared ownerless under duress is not regarded as ownerless, for we are not responsible to attend to the status of deceivers [poor who take what is in fact not due them]' [cf. T. Pe. 2:5]."

[E]   [Spelling out a different question,] There you say [along the lines of the sages' view], that what is declared ownerless property under duress is not regarded as ownerless property, while here you maintain that what is declared ownerless property under duress indeed is regarded as ownerless property.

[F]   Said R. Eleazar, "There it is declared ownerless property at the donor's own instance. But here, it is willy-nilly that he declares the *lulab* to be ownerless property."

[G]   Said R. Hananiah, son of R. Hillel, "And that is quite so. For you should know that in the present case the man already has in hand what is given in exchange for what he has handed over."

[H]   Rab instructed members of the house of R. Ahi, R. Hamnuna instructed the associates, "When you hand over a gift on the Festival [e.g., the *lulab* or *etrog*,] hand it over only with full and complete intent."

[I]   There is the following instance: R. Huna handed over an *etrog* as a gift to his son. He said to him, "If the actual Festival day is today, lo, it is a gift to you. If it is tomorrow, lo, it is a gift to you."

The Talmud takes up only M. 4:2E's provision, which it brings into juxtaposition with a parallel rule at T. Pe. 2:5. The text is somewhat odd. Jacob's question, so far as it relates to Dosa as against Judah, should address Judah's position. Judah holds that the declaration may be made even *after* the property has changed hands, while M. 4:2E wants the declaration to be made up front. Consequently, if at issue is the view of Judah (or Dosa), then the Mishnah cannot conform to the view of Judah. T. Pe. 2:5's version, which reverses opinions, therefore must be the one on which Y.'s discussion is based at **I.A**. There is a second curiosity, in that E spells out the question quite differently from **I.A–C**. That is, E sees the contradiction between the two passages to be based on sages' view, D, rather than on Dosa's or Judah's view, C. But matters are clear from there.

4:3

[A]   *The religious requirement of the willow branch: How so?*

[B]   *There was a place below Jerusalem, called Mosa. [People] go down there and gather young willow branches. They come and throw them along the sides of the altar, with their heads bent over the altar.*

[C]   *They blew on the shofar a sustained, a quavering, and a sustained note.*

[D]   *Every day they walk around the altar one time and say, "Save now, we beseech thee, O Lord! We beseech thee, O Lord, send now prosperity" (Ps. 118:25).*

[E]   *R. Judah says, "[They say,] 'Ani waho, save us we pray! Ani waho, save us we pray!'"*

[F]   *And on that day [the seventh day of the willow branch] they walk around the altar seven times.*

[G]   *When they leave, what do they say?*

[H]   *"Homage to you, O altar! Homage to you, O altar!"*

[I]   *R. Eliezer says, "For the Lord and for you, O altar! For the Lord and for you, O altar!"*

[I.A]   What is the meaning of the name, "Mosa"?

[B]   That it is excluded [from taxes].

[C]   Said R. Tanhuma, "It was called Qalonayya [Colonia]."

[II.A]   [As to the willow branches,] Bar Qappara said, "They were eleven cubits tall."

[B]   Said R. Yose, "The Mishnah has indicated that point: *With their heads bent over the altar [M. 4:3B].*"

[C]   R. Zeira sent and asked R. Daniel, son of R. Qatina, "Have you heard from your father whether it is necessary to say a blessing [along with the willow-rite], whether it is taken by itself, and whether it is subject to a minimum measurement [as to length]?"

[D]   R. Aibu bar Nigri in the name of R. Huna came and said, "[54c]
      It does require a blessing; it is taken by itself [not bound up
      with the other species], but as to whether or not a required mea-
      surement as to length applies to it I have not heard."

[E]   There they say R. Sheshet and R. Nahman bar Jacob: One said,
      "It must have three fresh twigs with leaves," and the other said,
      "Even a single twig [suffices]."

[III.A]   [As to walking around the altar,] it was taught: [Priests who are]
          maimed [participate in the procession].

[B]   R. Simeon b. Laqish asked before R. Yohanan, "Now will
      maimed priests enter the area between the porch and the altar?"

[C]   He said, "They were valid [for that purpose alone, but for no
      other]."

[IV.A]   R. Abbahu in the name of R. Yohanan: "This is how the Mishnah
         is to be read: 'Ani waho, *save us we pray!* Ani waho, *save us we
         pray [two times]' [M. 4 : 3E].*"

[B]   Said R. Abbahu, "'Stir up thy might and come to save us' (Ps.
      80 : 2) [is what R. Eliezer means to say, M. 4 : 3/I, that is], 'To
      you be all praise.'"

[V.A]   R. Ba Saronegayyah interpreted, "'And the Lord will give vic-
        tory to the tents of Judah first, [that the glory of the house of
        David and the glory of the inhabitants of Jerusalem may not be
        exalted over that of Judah]' (Zech. 12 : 7). It is written, 'And . . .
        give victory.'"

[B]   R. Zakkai interpreted, "'[Writhe and groan, O daughter of
      Zion, like a woman in travail;] for now you shall go forth from
      the city and dwell in the open country; [you shall go to Babylon.
      There you shall be rescued, there the Lord will redeem you from
      the hand of your enemies]' (Micah 4 : 10), 'My presence will be
      in the field.'"

[C]   Hananiah, son of the brother of R. Joshua says, "'I am the Lord
      your God, who brought you out of the land of Egypt, out of the
      house of bondage' (Ex. 20 : 2). It is written, 'You were taken out
      [too], [that is, God also was in bondage but was taken out].'"

[D]   R. Berekhiah, R. Jeremiah in the name of R. Hiyya bar Ba:
      "Levi bar Sisi interpreted in Nehardea as follows: 'And they
      saw the God of Israel; and there was under his feet as it were a

pavement of sapphire stone, like the very heaven for clearness'
(Ex. 24:10).

[E]   "That applies before they were redeemed. But after they were
redeemed, the brickwork was placed where the brick was gener-
ally kept. [That is, before Israel was redeemed, God had brickwork under his feet. He suffered along with Israel. After the
redemption the brickwork was cast away.]"

[F]   Said R. Berekhiah, "It is not written here, 'A brickwork of sapphire,' but, 'The *like* of a brickwork,' indicating that both it and
all the implements required for it were given; it and the basket
and the trowel pertaining to it were given."

[G]   Said R. Miashah, "In regard to Babylonia it is written, 'And
above the firmament over their heads there was the likeness of a
throne, in appearance like sapphire; and seated above the likeness of a throne was a likeness as it were of a human form'
(Ezek. 1:26).

[H]   "And in regard to Egypt, it is written, 'And they saw the God of
Israel; and there was under his feet as it were a pavement of
sapphire stone, like the very heaven for clearness' (Ex. 24:10).

[I]   "This serves to teach you that just as stone is tougher than brick,
so the subjugation to Babylonia was tougher than the subjugation to Egypt."

[J]   Bar Qappara taught, "Before Israel was redeemed from Egypt,
it was indicated in the firmament ['a pavement of sapphire
stone']. Once they were redeemed, it no longer appeared in the
firmament.

[K]   "What is the Scriptural evidence for this view? 'Like the very
heaven for clearness' (Ex. 24:10). This refers to the heaven
when it is clear of all clouds."

[L]   It has been taught in the name of R. Eliezer, "An idol passed
with Israel through the sea.

[M]   "What is the Scriptural basis for this statement? 'Whom thou
didst redeem for thyself from Egypt, nations and its gods'" (2
Sam. 7:23).

[N]   Said to him R. Aqiba, "Heaven forefend! If you say so, you
treat the holy as profane. What is the meaning of, 'Whom you

redeemed for yourself from Egypt'? It is as if you redeemed
yourself."

[VI.A]   *And on that day they walk around the altar seven times [M.
4:3F]:*

[B]   Said R. Aha, "This is a memorial to [the victory at] Jericho."

The point of the various exegeses of unit **V** is that God shares
the condition of Israel, as the statements of M. wish to emphasize.

4:4

[A]   *As the rite concerning it [is performed] on an ordinary day, so
the rite concerning it [is performed] on the Sabbath.*

[B]   *But they would gather [the willow branches] on Friday and leave
them in the gilded troughs [of water], so that they will not
wither.*

[C]   *R. Yohanan b. Beroqah says, "They would bring palm tufts and
beat them on the ground at the side of the altar,*

[D]   *"and that day was called the 'day of beating palm tufts.'"*

[E]   *Forthwith children throw away their* lulabs *and eat their* citrons.

[I.A]   [M. 4:4E] has said only, "Children." Lo, adults do not do so.

[B]   Did not R. Abina say in the name of Rab: "An *etrog* that was
invalidated on the first day of a Festival—it is permitted to eat
it"? [It is not set aside for a religious duty. In that case, why can
adults not do so?]

[C]   Said R. Yose, "[The reason is not that consideration at all.] There
[at M. 4:4E], the *etrog* is not suitable for the child to carry out
his religious obligations, but others may do so.

[D]   "But here [in the case of which Rab spoke], neither he nor any
one else may carry out his religious obligation with the invalid
etrog. [There is nothing to do with it, so it may be eaten.]"

The Talmud provides an acute reading of M. 4:4E.

4:5

[A]   *The Hallel psalms and the rejoicing [= peace-offerings of rejoic-*
      ing] are for eight days: How so?

[B]   *This rule teaches that a person is obligated for the Hallel psalms,*
      for the rejoicing [eating of peace-offerings], and for the honoring
      of the festival day,

[C]   *on the last festival day of the Festival,*

[D]   *just as he is on all the other days of the Festival.*

[E]   *The obligation to dwell in the sukkah for seven days: How so?*

[F]   *[If] one has finished eating [the last meal of the festival], he*
      should not untie his sukkah right away.

[G]   *But he brings down the utensils [only] from twilight onward—*

[H]   *on account of the honor due to the last festival day of the Festival.*

[I.A]   It was taught: **On eighteen days and one night do they recite**
        the *Hallel* psalms every year:

[B]   **The eight days of the Festival, the eight days of Hanukkah, the**
        Festival of Pentecost, and the first festival day of Passover and
        the night preceding it [T. Suk. 3:2A–B].

[II.A] R. Zeira, Ulla bar Ishmael in the name of R. Eleazar: "With [an
        animal designated as] peace-offerings for the festal offering,
        which one slaughtered on the eve of a festival [that is, prior to
        the festival day itself], one does not fulfill his obligation [to
        bring a festal offering] on the festival itself. [The slaughtering of
        the festal offering must take place at the time of the rejoicing on
        the festival itself, not prior to that time.]"

[B]   R. Ba objected, "Lo, it has been taught, 'With an animal desig-
        nated as a festal offering which one slaughtered on the four-
        teenth [of Nisan, that is, the day prior to the first festival day of
        Passover,] people carry out their obligation on the count of the
        offering of rejoicing required for Passover. [This festal offering is
        slaughtered along with the Passover-offering, that is, prior to
        sundown on the fourteenth of Nisan.]' Now do they not carry
        out their obligation with that animal on the count of peace-
        offerings?"

[C]   Said R. Zeira, "Interpret that statement to speak of a case in which [one postponed] slaughtering the animal until the festival day itself."

[D]   [But, since the time of slaughtering it has passed, the beast falls into the category of peace-offerings,] R. Ba said to him, "If they slaughtered it on the festival, this no longer serves as a festal offering on the fourteenth [of Nisan, accompanying the Passover, such as is required]."

[E]   What is the upshot of the matter? [Do people carry out their obligation on the count of bringing peace-offerings as a festal offering?]

[F]   Said R. Zeira, "When I was over there [in Babylonia], I heard Ulla bar Ishmael teach in the name of R. Eleazar, while when I came up here, I heard the teaching taught by R. Hiyya in the name of R. Eleazar: 'So that you will be altogether joyful' (Deut. 16 : 15). The use of the word 'altogether' serves to encompass the night of [following QH:] the last day of the Festival, including that night within the season of rejoicing. [At that time the festal offering may be slaughtered to fulfill one's obligation for the festival.]"

[G]   "Or is it possible to maintain that the language also serves the purpose of including the first night of the festival?

[H]   "Scripture has said, 'Altogether,' serving to differentiate.

[I]   R. Hiyya in the name of R. Eleazar: "'And you shall rejoice in your feast' (Deut. 16 : 14). Since you are liable for a festal offering, you are liable for an offering of rejoicing. [One is not liable on the first night of a festival for a festal offering, therefore one is not liable to slaughter at that time an offering of rejoicing.]"

[J]   They objected, "Lo, we have learned: *[The recitation of] the Hallel psalms and the rejoicing[-offering] are for eight days [M. 4:5A].* Now what if the first day of the festival should coincide with the Sabbath? [The festal offering cannot be slaughtered that day.] As to slaughtering the festal offering on the eve of the festival, [that is, on Friday,] one is not permitted to do so either, for R. Zeira has said, Ulla bar Ishmael in the name of R. Eleazar stated, 'With peace-offerings brought as a festal offering which one slaughtered on the eve of the festival one cannot carry out his obligation for a festal offering for the festival itself.'

[K] "As to slaughtering the animal on the festival, that too you cannot do, for we have indeed learned that a festal offering does not override the prohibitions of the Sabbath.

[L] "So under what circumstances have they stated that the recitation of the *Hallel* psalms and the rejoicing[-offering] can go on for eight days?"

[M] Said R. Yose, "R. Abodemi, who would go down to Babylonia, interpreted the passage to speak of priests, who could offer a goat [offered on the festival day, through which they would carry out their obligation to eat a rejoicing-offering] [M. Hag. 1:4C]."

[III.A] [As to M. 4:5F,] R. Abba bar Kahana, R. Hiyya bar Ashi in the name of Rab: "A person has to invalidate his *sukkah* while it is still day [on the seventh day of the Festival, if he proposes to eat in it on the Eighth Day of Solemn Assembly, so that he will not appear to be eating in the *sukkah* and so adding to the Festival itself]. [By invalidating the *sukkah*, he indicates that he realizes he is not adding a day to the Festival but observing a separate festival, the Eighth Day of Solemn Assembly.]"

[B] R. Joshua b. Levi said, "[In any event,] he has to say the Sanctification of the day in his house [not in the *sukkah*]."

[C] R. Jacob bar Aha in the name of Samuel: "If one said the Sanctification in one house and decided to eat in some other house, he has to say the Sanctification [again]."

[D] R. Aha, R. Hinena in the name of Rab: "He who finds his *sukkah* pleasant says the Sanctification on the night of the final festival day in his house, then he goes up and eats in his *sukkah*." [This contradicts C.]

[E] Said R. Abin, "And they do not differ about this matter, for Rab [D] said what he said in a case in which the man did not intend to eat in some other house, while Samuel said [C] that if he intended to eat in some other house [he has to say the Sanctification again]."

[F] [No, they differ, for,] said R. Mana, "The statement of Samuel accords with R. Hiyya [A], and the statement of R. Hoshaiah accords with the view of R. Joshua b. Levi [B]."

[G] Said R. Imi, "That is to say that they disputed about this matter explicitly."

The point of M. 4:5A–B is that the Eighth Day of Assembly requires the rites of *Hallel* psalms and rejoicing (offering peace-offerings, eating meat). M. 4:5D–F explain that the *sukkah* is left standing all seven days and not dismantled until after the closing festival. Unit **I** makes a trivial observation. Unit **II** is primary to Y. Hag. 1:4 and is not demanded by the present passage of the Mishnah. Unit **III** intersects with M. 4:5F, dismantling the *sukkah* prior to the Eighth Day of Solemn Assembly, not regarded as part of the Festival at all. On the interpretation of **III**.F see PM. **III**.G makes sense only at Y. Ber. 6:6, to which the whole is primary.

4:6 (L + V: 4:6–8)

[A]   *The water libation—for seven days: How so?*

[B]   *A golden flask, holding three logs in volume, did one fill with water from Siloam.*

[C]   *[When] they reached the Water Gate, they blow a sustained, a quavering, and a sustained blast on the ram's horn.*

[D]   *[The priest] went on the ramp [at the south] and turned to his left [southwest].*

[E]   *There were two silver bowls there.*

[F]   *R. Judah says, "They were of plaster, but they had darkened because of the wine."*

[G]   *They were perforated with holes like a narrow snout,*

[H]   *one wide, one narrow,* .

[I]   *so that both of them would be emptied together [one of its wine, flowing slowly, the other of its water, flowing quickly].*

[J]   *The one on the west was for water, the one on the east was for wine.*

[K]   *[If] he emptied the flask of water into the bowl for wine, and the flask of wine into the bowl for water, he has nonetheless carried out the rite.*

[L]   *R. Judah says, "A log [of water] would one pour out as the water libation all eight days."*

[M]   *And to the one who pours out the water libation they say, "Lift up your hand [so that we can see the water pouring out]!"*

[N]   *For one time one [priest] poured out the water on his feet.*

[O]   *And all the people stoned him with their citrons.*

[I.A] "[They sound the *shofar*, M. 4:6C,] said R. Yose b. Haninah, "so as to publicize the matter."

[B]   Yose b. Haninah in the name of Menahem of Jodapata: "[That the water libation was to be three *log*s in volume] represents the position of R. Aqiba, who maintained that the water libation derives from the authority of the Torah [and, by analogy to the one for wine, must be three *log*s in volume]."

[C]   There we learned: *R. Eleazar says, "Also: He who pours a water libation on the Festival outside [of the Temple] is liable [on the count of a cultic act outside of the Temple] [M. Zeb. 13:6]."*

[D]   Said R. Yohanan, "The entire theory of R. Eleazar accords with the one of R. Aqiba, his master.

[E]   "Just as R. Aqiba has said, 'The water libation derives from the authority of the Torah,' so R. Eleazar has said, 'The water libation derives from the authority of the Torah, [and that is why it must be done only in the Temple].'"

[F]   [The statements that follow see a point of difference concerning the view of Eleazar.] What is the difference between the [Tannas, whose traditions follow]:

[G]   There is a Tanna who teaches in the name of R. Eleazar, "It is necessary that the drawing of the water be for the purpose of the [water-offering of] the Festival."

[H]   There is a Tanna who teaches in the name of R. Eleazar, "It is not necessary that the drawing of the water be for the purpose of the Festival."

[I]   He who says that it is necessary that the drawing of the water be for the sake of the Festival maintains that R. Eleazar accords with R. Aqiba [that the rite derives from the authority of the Torah].

[J]   He who says that it is not necessary that the drawing of the water be for the sake of the Festival maintains that R. Eleazar accords with rabbis [who do not regard the rite as deriving from the authority of the Torah]. [Hence the issue of designation of water for this rite is moot.]

[K]   No, that is an impossible proposition. For R. Yohanan said, "The entire theory of R. Eleazar accords with the one of R. Aqiba, his master.

[L]   "Just as R. Aqiba has said, 'The water libation derives from the authority of the Torah,' so R. Eleazar has said, 'The water libation derives from the authority of the Torah.'"

[M]   Then what is at issue [between the Tannas whose traditions are cited at G–H]?

[N]   Said R. Zeira, "It is the case of one who poured out a libation of three *logs* inside the Temple, and three *logs* outside the Temple.

[O]   "There is a Tanna who teaches, 'The water is subject to a maximum measure of volume,' and there is a Tanna who teaches, 'The water is not subject to a maximum measure of volume.'

[P]   "He who has said that the water is subject to a maximum measure of volume declares the man exempt [for pouring out the water outside of the Temple, since he already has done so inside the Temple, and so carried out the required rite]. [What he did outside is null.]

[Q]   "He who has said that the water is not subject to a maximum measure of volume declares the man liable [for pouring out the water outside of the Temple, since, whatever he does in one place, what he does in the other is equally valid]. [There is no point at which one necessarily has carried out the obligation of the water libation.]"

[II.A]   Yose bar Asyan in the name of R. Simeon b. Laqish: "The bowls have to be stopped up at the time of the libation.

[B]   "What is the scriptural basis for this position?

[C]   "'Its drink offering shall be a fourth of a *hin* for each lamb; in the holy place you shall pour out a drink offering [54d] of strong drink to the Lord'" (Num. 28:7).

[III.A]   It has been taught: **R. Yose says, "The cavity of the Pits was perforated down to the abyss.**

[B]   **"What is the scriptural basis for this view?**

[C]   "'He digged it and cleared it of stones, and planted it with choice vines; he built a watchtower in the midst of it, and hewed out a wine vat in it; and he looked for it to yield grapes, but it yielded wild grapes' (Is. 5:2).

[D]   "'He built a watchtower in the midst of it'—this refers to the Temple.

[E]   "'He hewed out a wine vat in it'—this refers to the altar.

[F]   "'And also a wine vat . . .'—this refers to the cavity" [T. Suk. 3:15C–F].

[G]   R. Simeon says, "[The pits] were the work of Heaven [at the creation of the world]."

[H]   Since the pits were the work of Heaven, is it possible that they should not be well built, as would be the work of a craftsman?

[I]   Scripture says, "Your rounded thighs are like jewels, the work of a master hand" (Song 7:2).

[J]   They were better built than the work of a craftsman.

[K]   It has been taught: **R. Eliezer b. R. Sadoq says, "There was a small passageway between the ascent and the altar at the west side of the ramp.**

[L]   "Once every seventy years the young priests would go down there and gather up the congealed wine, which looked like circles of pressed figs, and they burned it in a state of sanctity, as it is said, 'In the holy place shall you pour out a drink offering of strong drink unto the Lord' (Num. 28:7).

[M]   "Just as the pouring out must be in a state of sanctity, thus the burning of it must be in a state of sanctity" [T. Suk. 3:15].

[N]   [Commenting on Num. 28:7, cited above, L,] Rabbi said, "Notice how the Torah has seized upon language expressing desire, satisfaction, and strong drink."

[O]   R. Judah bar Laqorah in the name of R. Samuel bar Nahman: "When the Temple was destroyed, wine jelly ceased to be available, and white glass ceased to be used."

[P]   What is white glass?

[Q]   It is cut glass.

[**IV**.A] [As to M. 4:6G–H:] They proposed to state, "The wide one was for water, the narrow one for wine."

[B] For R. Jonah in the name of R. Imi said, "A hole that will not let water pass will let wine pass, and one that will not let wine pass will let oil pass, and one that will not let oil pass will let honey pass."

[C] And even if you should state that the matter is opposite [so the wide one was for wine, the narrow one for water], it accords with the view of R. Judah.

[D] *For R. Judah said, "A log of water would one pour out as the water libation all eight days" [M. 4:6L].*

[**V**.A] R. Simeon b. Laqish asked before R. Yohanan, "If one carried out the libation-offering before the sacrifice [of the daily whole offering], what is the rule?

[B] "If one poured out the water libation by night, what is the rule?

[C] "If one did not pour out the water libation on one day, what is the law as to doing so on the next day?"

[D] He said to him, "Let us derive the answer from the following:

[E] "R. Ila said in the name of R. Yose, 'And its libations . . .' (Num. 29:31)—[the plural indicates] one for the water libations and the other for the wine libations.'

[F] "That indicates, If one carried out the libation-offering before the sacrifice [of the daily whole-offering], it is valid.

[G] "If one poured out the water libation by night, it is valid.

[H] "If one did not pour out the water libation on one day, he should not pour out a water libation [for that same purpose] on the next day,

[I] "on the principle that if the day has passed, the offering pertaining to that day has passed also."

[**VI**.A] [With reference to M. 4:1C, the water libation is for seven days, and Judah says, "It is for eight days"; and M. 4:6L, "There was a water libation of a *log*," while sages say, "Three *log*s," so M. 4:6B, we may then observe, in T.'s formulation:] **You turn out to rule, He who wants more water diminishes the number** of days, and he who wants more days diminishes the volume of the water [T. Suk. 3:16K].

[VII.A] There is he who proposes to state: "[The one who poured the water on his feet, M. 4:6N] is the same priest who misbehaved in connection with the burning of the red cow [at T. Par. 3:8, a Sadducee who rejected the conception of the law], and is also the same one who misbehaved in connection with the rite of the Day of Atonement [at Y. Yoma 1:5, burning the incense outside and bringing it inside the Holy of Holies]. [All three incidents were the work of one Sadducean priest.]"

[B] R. Simon did not hold that view, but he maintained either that the one responsible for the misconduct with the red cow and the one responsible for the misconduct at the rite of the Festival is one priest, while the one of the Day of Atonement is another,

[C] or that the one involving the red cow and the rite of the Day of Atonement was one and the same man, while the one involved with the rite of the Festival was another.

[D] He who has said that there were not many days before [the one who did things in the wrong way on the Day of Atonement] died holds that the same man did all three deeds [one on the Day of Atonement; between then and the Festival he burned the red cow in the wrong status as to uncleanness, then on the Festival he poured the water-offering onto his feet and was stoned and died].

[E] He who said that worms came out of his nose, and there was something like the footprint of a calf on his forehead, [so he died immediately,] maintains the view that either the one involved in the incident of the red cow and of the Festival was one priest, while the one involved on the Day of Atonement was a different priest,

[F] or the one involved in the incident of the red cow and the Day of Atonement was one priest, and the incident involving the Festival was another priest.

[VIII.A] [With reference to M. 4:6N–O,] The courtyard cried out, "Get out of here! Get out of here, sons of Eli! For you have contaminated the house of our God."

[B] On that day [now following T.'s text:] the horn of the altar was damaged, so the sacred service was annulled for that day, until they brought a lump of salt and put it on it, so that the altar should not appear to be damaged.

[C]   For any altar lacking a horn, ramp, or foundation is invalid.

[D]   [Y. lacks:] R. Yose b. R. Judah says, "Also the rim" [T. Suk. 3:16D–F].

[IX.A]   ["Reverting to the story of VII.E, that the priest on the Day of Atonement had a footprint of a calf on his forehead, where could it have come from?"] they asked before R. Abbahu, "For lo, it is written, 'There shall be no man in the tent of meeting when he enters to make atonement in the holy place until he comes out' (Lev. 16:17).

[B]   "That covers even those concerning whom it is written, 'As for the likeness of their faces, each had the face of a man in front; the four had the face of a lion on the right side, the four had the face of an ox on the left side, and the four had the face of an eagle at the back' (Ezek. 1:10). Even these should not be in the tent of meeting when he enters to make atonement for the holy."

[C]   He said to them, "That [Lev. 16:17] applies when he goes in in the proper manner [but not when he has put incense into his hand before going in]."

The important issue of unit I should not be missed in the rather formalistic discussion into which it is cast. It concerns the origins of the water libation. The emphasis is that the rite derives from the law of the Torah. There are some textual problems, particularly at I.F. Units II, III complement M. with T.'s pertinent materials. III.L in T.'s version cites Num. 28:7. Y.'s version omits reference to the verse. Since III.N assumes that that verse has been cited, it is clear that the Talmud's discussion presupposes T.'s text, and not what is now before us in Y. Unit IV glosses M., as indicated. Unit V begins to expand the matter by reference to more theoretical problems. Unit VI draws together two distinct passages, as indicated. Unit VII takes up the identity of the priest at issue in M., as against other recalcitrant priests known to the Mishnah and the Tosefta. Unit VIII reverts to M.'s tale, and unit IX resumes the discussion of unit VII.

4:7 (L + V: 4:9)

[A]   *As the rite concerning it [was carried out] on an ordinary day, so was the rite [carried out] on the Sabbath.*

[B]   *But on the eve of the Sabbath one would fill with water from Siloam a gold jug which was not sanctified,*

[C]   *and he would leave it in a chamber [in the Temple].*

[D]   *[If] it was poured out or left uncovered, one would fill the jug from the laver [in the courtyard].*

[E]   *For wine and water which have been left uncovered are invalid for the altar.*

[I.A]   What difference does it make to me that the gold jug [M. 4:7B] was not sanctified? Even if it had been sanctified, [it should be acceptable]. [The man may pour the water in with the intent that the water not be regarded as sanctified. The concern of M. 4:7B is that if the water should be sanctified by the jug, then it will be invalidated by being left overnight.]

[B]   For did not R. Aha, R. Hinena in the name of R. Yose say, "'You shall also anoint the altar of burnt offering and all its utensils, and consecrate the altar; and the altar shall be most holy' (Ex. 40:10)?

[C]   "Just as the altar only effects sanctification through one's knowledge and intent, also utensils used for the altar will not effect sanctification except with knowledge and intent. [Accordingly, even if water is left in a sanctified vessel, it will not be regarded as sanctified, since the priest's intention is not that the water be sanctified by the utensil in which it is kept overnight.]"

[D]   Hezekiah said, "It is so that people should not say, 'We saw water that was drawn for the sanctification [washing] of hands and feet rendered invalid by being kept overnight.'"

[E]   Members of the house of R. Yannai say, "It is so that people will not say, 'We saw water drawn for the Festival['s libation-offering] invalidated by being kept overnight [prior to use].'"

[F]   R. Yohanan said, "It is for appearance's sake."

[G]   Now we do not know whether it was [for appearance's sake] in line with what Hezekiah said, or whether it was [for appearance's sake] in line with what R. Yannai's representative said.

[H]   It represents a judgment based on the opinions of all parties.

[II.A]   R. Pedat in the name of R. Hoshaiah: "Water used for the rite of the accused wife is invalidated if left standing overnight."

[B]   R. Aha in the name of R. Abina, "Any sort of material, part of which is not destined for the altar itself, is in no way rendered invalid by being left overnight."

[III.A]   [As to M. 4 : 7E, wine and water left uncovered may not be used for the altar,] they proposed to rule, "If one transgressed and brought [such wine or water], it is valid."

[B]   R. Joshua, the Southerner, taught before R. Jonah, that water and wine left uncovered are invalid for use on the altar.

[C]   What is the scriptural basis for that view?

[D]   "And one sheep from every flock of two hundred from the watering places of Israel" (Ezek. 45 : 15). It derives from something which is permitted for use in Israel. [This excludes water left uncovered, which people may not drink.]

[E]   Up to this point we have dealt with water. How about wine?

[F]   Said R. Shobetai, "'. . . which cheers God and man . . .' (Judges 9 : 13). [What man may drink may be given to God on the altar.]"

Unit I explains the detail of M. 4 : 7B. Unit II is tacked on. Unit III then clarifies the rule of M. 4 : 7E and its scriptural foundations.

5 Yerushalmi Sukkah Chapter Five

5:1

[A] [55a] *Flute playing is for five or six days:*

[B] *This refers to the flute playing on* bet hashshoebah,

[C] *which overrides the restrictions of neither the Sabbath nor of a festival day.*

[D] *They said: Anyone who has not seen the rejoicing of* bet hashshoebah *in his life has never seen rejoicing.*

[I.A] Lo, [the flute playing] that accompanies the offering overrides [the prohibitions of the Sabbath, but otherwise, it does not].

[B] The Mishnah therefore has been formulated in accord with the view of R. Yose b. R. Judah.

[C] For it has been taught: "The playing of the flute along with the offering overrides the restrictions of the Sabbath," the words of R. Yose b. R. Judah.

[D] And sages say, "It does not override the restrictions of either the Sabbath or the festival."

[E] There we have learned: *On twelve days in the year the flute was played before the altar: on the occasion of slaughtering the first Passover-offering [on the fifteenth of Nisan], on the occasion of slaughtering the second Passover-offering [on the fifteenth of Iyyar], on the first festival day of Passover, on the festival day of Pentecost, and on the eight days of the Feast [Tabernacles] [M. Ar. 2:3].* Now can there be eight days without a Sabbath? [How can there be flute playing on all eight days, as M. Ar. 2:3 has said, as against M. 5:1A–C?]

[F]   R. Yose stated the following matter without specifying an authority, while R. Yose bar Bun said in the name of R. Yohanan, "It represents the view of R. Yose b. R. Judah." [The foregoing assumes T.'s version of **I.**C, rather than that given above at **I.**C. T.'s version is as follows: "**Flute playing overrides the restrictions of the Sabbath,**" **the words of R. Yose b. R. Judah. And sages say, "It does not override the restrictions even of the festival day"** (T. Suk. 4:14A–B).]

[G]   In the view of those rabbis [who differ from Yose b. R. Judah], why does the flute playing not override the restrictions of the Sabbath?

[H]   It is because it is not clear [from the Scripture that there should be such a rite].

[I]   And lo, it is written, "And all the people went up after him, playing on pipes, and rejoicing with great joy, so that the earth was split by their noise" (1 Kings 1:40).

[J]   The Scripture speaks of the rejoicing in connection with Solomon [and not the Festival].

[**II.**A]   R. Jonah in the name of R. Ba bar Mamel: "'You shall have a song as in the night when a holy feast is kept; and gladness of heart, as when one sets out to the sound of the flute to go to the mountain of the Lord, to the Rock of Israel' (Is. 30:29). So long as the flute playing is practiced, the *Hallel* psalms are part of the custom as well."

[B]   R. Yose b. R. Bun in the name of R. Ba bar Mamel: "Why do they recite the *Hallel* psalms all seven days of the Festival? It is on account of the *lulab,* which is renewed every day."

[C]   And why do we have to seek these several teachings in respect to the flute playing?

[D]   We have learned that this comes at specified times, and that comes at specified times.

[E]   This is beloved and that is beloved.

[F]   So they have made what is beloved depend upon what is beloved.

[G]   [Along these same lines as F,] on Pentecost one says to [the priest], "Here is unleavened bread for you, here is leavened bread for you."

[H]   There is a Tanna who teaches, "Here is leavened bread for you, here is unleavened bread for you."

[I]   He who said, "Here is unleavened bread" [first] holds that it is more desired.

[J]   He who said, "Here is leavened bread" holds that it is offered more regularly, [and therefore takes precedence].

[III.A]   Said R. Joshua b. Levi, "Why is it called *bet hashshoebah* [place of drawing]?

[B]   "For from there they draw the Holy Spirit, in line with the following verse of Scripture, 'With joy you will draw water from the wells of salvation'" (Is. 12:3).

[IV.A]   There is the following story: R. Levi and Judah bar Nahman were collecting two *sela*s [a week] to gather together a congregation before R. Yohanan.

[B]   R. Levi entered and preached, "Jonah the son of Amittai came from the tribe of Asher, for it is written, 'Asher did not drive out the inhabitants of Acco nor the inhabitants of Sidon' (Judges 1:31).

[C]   "And it is written, 'Arise, go to Zarephath, which belongs to Sidon, and dwell there. Behold, I have commanded a widow there to feed you'" (I Kings 17:9).

[D]   R. Yohanan went up and preached, "Jonah b. Amittai came from the tribe of Zebulun, for it is written, 'The third lot came up for the tribe of Zebulun, according to its families. And the territory of its inheritance reached as far as Sarid' (Josh. 19:10).

[E]   "And it is written, 'Thence it goes to Daberath, then up to Japhia; from there it passes along on the east toward the sunrise to Gath-hepher, to Eth-kazin, and going on to Rimmon it bends toward Neah' (Josh. 19:13).

[F]   "And it is written, 'He restored the border of Israel from the entrance of Hamath as far as the Sea of the Arabah, according to the word of the Lord, the God of Israel, which he spoke by his servant Jonah the son of Amittai, the prophet, who was from Gath-hepher'" (2 Kings 14:25).

[G]   On another Sabbath, said R. Levi to Judah bar Nahman, "Take these two *sela*s and go, gather the congregation before R.

Yohanan." He went in and said before them, "Correctly did R. Yohanan teach us. His mother came from Asher, while his father came from Zebulun. 'Zebulun shall dwell at the shore of the sea; he shall become a haven for ships, and his border shall be at Sidon' (Gen. 49:13).

[H]   "An offshoot that went forth from him was from Sidon.

[I]   "And it is written, 'He went down to Joppa'" (Jonah 1:3).

[J]   Was it not necessary to say, "He went down to Acco"?

[K]   Said R. Jonah, "Jonah b. Amittai was one of those who came up for the festivals [to Jerusalem], and he came in for the rejoicing of *bet hashshoebah*, and the Holy Spirit rested on him.

[L]   "This serves to teach you that the Holy Spirit rests only on someone whose heart is happy.

[M]   "What is the scriptural basis for this view? 'But now bring me a minstrel. And when the minstrel played, the power of the Lord came upon him'" (2 Kings 3:15).

[N]   Said R. Benjamin bar Levi, "It is not written here, 'And when the minstrel played,' but rather, 'And when the harp played [on its own].'" [This serves Y. Ber. 1:1 and has no place here.]

[V.A] It has been taught [in T.'s version]: **Said R. Judah, "Whoever has never seen the double-colonnade [the basilica-synagogue] of Alexandria in Egypt has never seen Israel's glory in his entire life.**

[B]   **"It was a kind of large basilica, with one colonnade inside another.**

[C]   **"Sometimes there were [55b] twice as many people there as those who went forth from Egypt.**

[D]   **"Now there were seventy-one [Y.: seventy] golden thrones set up there, one for each of the seventy-one elders, each one worth twenty-five talents of gold, with a wooden platform in the middle.**

[E]   **"The minister of the synagogue stands on it, with flags in his hand. When one began to read, the other would wave the flags so the people would answer, 'Amen,' for each and every blessing. Then that one would wave the flags, and they would answer, 'Amen.'**

[F]   "They did not sit in a jumble, but the goldsmiths sat by them-selves, the silversmiths by themselves, the weavers by themselves, the bronze-workers by themselves, and the black-smiths by themselves.

[G]   "All this why? So that when a traveller came along, [he could find his fellow craftsmen,] and on that basis he could gain a living" [T. Suk. 4:6].

[H]   And who destroyed it all? It was the evil Trajan.

[VI.A]   R. Simeon b. Yohai taught, "The Israelites were warned at three points not to go back to the Land of Egypt.

[B]   "For it is said, 'And Moses said to the people, Fear not, stand firm, and see the salvation of the Lord, which he will work for you today; for the Egyptians whom you see today, you shall never see again' (Ex. 14:13).

[C]   "'Since the Lord has said to you, You shall never return that way again' (Deut. 17:16).

[D]   "'And the Lord will bring you back in ships to Egypt, a journey which I promised that you should never make again; and there you shall offer yourselves for sale to your enemies as male and female slaves, but no man will buy you' (Deut. 28:68).

[E]   "In all three instances they did go back, and in those three in-stances they fell.

[F]   "Once in the time of Sennacherib, king of Assyria, as it is said, 'Woe to those who go down to Egypt for help and rely on horses, who trust in chariots because they are many and in horsemen because they are very strong, but do not look to the Holy One of Israel or consult the Lord!' (Is. 31:1).

[G]   "What is written thereafter? 'The Egyptians are men, and not God; and their horses are flesh, and not spirit. When the Lord stretches out his hand, the helper will stumble, and he who is helped will fall, and they will all perish together' (Is. 31:3).

[H]   "Once in the time of Yohanan b. Qorah: 'Then the sword which you fear shall overtake you there in the land of Egypt; and the famine of which you are afraid shall follow hard after you to Egypt; and there you shall die'" (Jer. 42:16).

[VII.A]   In the time of Tronianus, the evil one, a son was born to him on the ninth of Ab, and [the Israelites] were fasting.

[B]   His daughter died on Hanukkah, and [the Israelites] lit candles.

[C]   His wife sent a message to him, saying, "Instead of going out to conquer the barbarians, come and conquer the Jews, who have rebelled against you."

[D]   He thought that the trip would take ten days, but he came in five.

[E]   He came and found the Israelites occupied in study of the Light [Torah], with the following verse: "The Lord will bring a nation against you from afar, from the end of the earth, as swift as the eagle flies, a nation whose language you do not understand" (Deut. 28:49).

[F]   He said to them, "With what are you occupied?"

[G]   They said to him, "With thus-and-so."

[H]   He said to them, "That man [I] thought that it would take ten days to make the trip, and I arrived in five days." His legions surrounded them and killed them.

[I]   He said to the women, "Obey my legions, and I shall not kill you."

[J]   They said to him, "What you did to the ones who have fallen do also to us who are yet standing."

[K]   He mingled their blood with the blood of their men, until the blood flowed into the ocean as far as Cyprus.

[L]   At that moment the horn of Israel was cut off, and it is not destined to return to its place until the son of David will come.

Since the celebration does not override the prohibitions of the Sabbath, if the first festival day of the Festival does not coincide with the Sabbath, then the Sabbath comes on an intermediate day of the festival, leaving five days for the flute playing; but if the first festival day of the Festival coincides with the Sabbath, then there will be six ordinary days on which the celebration may take place, so much for A–C. The celebration described at M. 5:1 Dff. has nothing to do with the flute playing. Unit I seeks the authority behind M.'s rule. We note that Y.'s version at I.C is appropriate to the discourse of I.A–B, while T.'s version of I.C is appropriate to I.D–F. Unit II deals with the relationship of flute playing and the *Hallel* psalms. Unit III is the last constituent of the Talmud directly related to the Mishnah. But all that follows belongs. For unit **V** takes up the rhetorical form of M. 5:1A. I assume that unit **VI** is inserted because it deals with Israelites in Egypt, the topic of unit **V**. Unit **VII**, likewise, is joined because it amplifies **V.H.** Hence we may account for nearly the entire construction, excluding only unit **IV**.

5:2

[A]   *At the end of the first festival day of the Festival [the priest and Levites] went down to the woman's courtyard.*

[B]   *And they made a major enactment [by putting men below and women above].*

[C]   *And there were golden candle holders there, with four gold bowls on their tops, and four ladders for each candle stick.*

[D]   *And four young apprentice-priests with jars of oil containing a hundred and twenty logs, [would climb up the ladders and] pour [the oil] into each bowl.*

[I.A]   [In T.'s version:] **Said R. Joshua b. Hananiah, "In all the days of celebrating bet hashshoebah, we never saw a moment of sleep.**

[B]   **"We would get up in time for the morning daily whole-offering.**

[C]   **"From there we would go to the synagogue, from there to the additional offerings [in the Temple], from there to eating and drinking, from there to the study house, from there to the Temple to see the evening's daily whole-offering, from there to the celebration of the rejoicing of bet hashshoebah"** [T. Suk. 4:5].

[D]   And lo, it has been taught: [If someone said,] "By an oath! I shall not sleep for three days"—they flog him [for taking an oath he cannot keep], and he may sleep immediately. [How can Joshua claim that people did not sleep for days on end?]

[E]   They would doze off.

[II.A]   *And they made a major enactment [M. 5:2B]:*

[B]   What was this enactment that they made there?

[C]   It was that they set up the men by themselves and the women by themselves.

[D]   That is in line with what we have learned there: *In the beginning the [women's court] was empty, but they surrounded it with a gallery, so that the women would look on from above, and the men below, so that they should not mingle together [M. Mid. 2:5].*

[E]   Whence did they learn this rule?

[F]   From a teaching of the Torah: "The land shall mourn, each family by itself; the family of the house of David by itself, and their wives by themselves; the family of the house of Nathan by itself, and their wives by themselves" (Zech. 12:12).

[G]   [Interpreting the verse just now cited, there were] two Amoras. One said, "This refers to a lamentation for the Messiah."

[H]   The other said, "This refers to a lamentation for the evil impulse."

[I]   He who said, "This refers to a lamentation for the Messiah": now if at a time at which they are in mourning, you have said, "The men must be by themselves and the women by themselves," when they are rejoicing, is it not an argument *a fortiori!*

[J]   He who said, "This refers to a lamentation for the evil impulse": now if at a time at which they are not subject to the evil impulse, you have said, "The men must be by themselves and the women by themselves," when they are subject to the evil impulse, is it not an argument *a fortiori!*

[III.A]   *There were golden candle holders there [M. 5:2C]:*

[B]   Bar Qappara said, "And they were a hundred cubits high."

[C]   And lo, it has been taught: Whatever is a hundred cubits high has to be thirty-three cubits broad at the base.

[D]   Now with a ladder on this side and a ladder on that side [M. 5:2C], each taking up thirty-three cubits, [the area required for the ladder on either side and the base would be sixty-six cubits for each lamp].

[E]   Now it has been taught: *The Temple Court was in all a hundred and eighty-seven cubits long and a hundred and thirty-five cubits wide [M. Mid. 5:1A].* [Two candle holders, therefore, would fill up 132 cubits alone, and with the space taken up by the ladders, 136 cubits. The courtyard would not be sufficiently wide for such an arrangement.]

[F]   There is a teaching: The place in which they stood was subject to a miracle.

[IV.A]   What is the meaning of: *With jars of oil . . . [M. 5:2D]?*

[B]   Does it mean that all of them together had a hundred and twenty *log*s of oil,

[C]   or each one of them individually had a hundred and twenty *log*s of oil? [This question is not answered.]

Unit **I** carries forward the discussion pertinent to M. 5:1. Units **II, III,** and **IV** amplify the statements of M., as indicated.

5:3

[A]   *Out of the worn-out undergarments and girdles of the priests they made wicks,*

[B]   *and with them they lit the candlesticks.*

[C]   *And there was not a courtyard in Jerusalem which was not lit up from the light of* bet hashshoebah.

[I.A]   It has been taught: Out of the worn-out undergarments of the high priest they kindled the lamps that were inside [the Temple], and out of the worn-out undergarments of the ordinary priests they kindled the lamps that were outside [in the courtyard].

[II.A]   Said R. Samuel bar R. Isaac, "It is written, '[And you shall command the people of Israel that they bring to you pure beaten olive oil for the light,] that a lamp may be set up to burn continually' (Ex. 27:20).

[B]   "They determined that you have nothing that produces a good flame except for a wick of linen."

[III.A]   What is the meaning of the word for *they made wicks* [at M. 5:3A]?

[B]   R. Haggai interpreted it before R. Yose, "They make wicks of them."

[IV.A]   It was taught: *There was not a courtyard in Jerusalem which was not lit up from the light of* bet hashshoebah *[M. 5:3C].*

[B]   It was taught: A woman can sift wheat by the light of the fire [of the Temple pile].

[C]   And was this not regarded as violating the laws of sacrilege?

[D]   No, for R. Joshua b. Levi said, "Smell, sight, sound—they are not subject to the laws of sacrilege."

[V.A]   There were six sounds that they could hear from Jericho:

[B]   *From Jericho did they hear the sound of the great gate opening. From Jericho did they hear the sound of the shovel. From Jericho did they hear the sound of the wooden device which Ben Qatin made for the laver. From Jericho did they hear the sound of Gabini, the crier. From Jericho did they hear the sound of the flute. From Jericho did they hear the sound of the cymbal. There are those who say, "Also the voice of the high priest when he made mention of the divine Name on the Day of Atonement." From Jericho they could smell the scent of the compounding of the incense. Said R. Eleazar b. Diglai, "My father's house and goats were on the mountain of Mikhwar, and they sneezed from the smell of the compounding of the incense" [M. Tam. 3:8, omitting M. Tam. 3:8G–H, which would have made eight, rather than six sounds].*

Unit **I** expands on M. 5:3A. Unit **II** deals with materials suitable for wicks. Units **III** and **IV** lightly gloss M. The inclusion of unit **V** is inexplicable.

5:4

[A]   *The pious men and wonder-workers would dance before them with flaming torches in their hand,*

[B]   *and they would sing before them songs and praises.*

[C]   *And the Levites beyond counting played on harps, lyres, cymbals, trumpets, and [other] musical instruments,*

[D]   *[standing, as they played] on the fifteen steps which go down from the Israelites' court to the women's court—*

[E]   *corresponding to the fifteen Songs of Ascents which are in the Book of Psalms—*

[F]   *on these the Levites stand with their instruments and sing their song.*

[I.A]   *The pious men and wonder-workers [M. 5:4A]:*

[B]   [In T.'s version:] **What did they sing?**

[C]   **"Happy is he who has not sinned. But all who have sinned will He forgive."**

[D]   **And some of them say, "Fortunate is my youth, which did not bring my old age into shame"—these [who say this song] are the wonder-workers.**

[E]   **And some of them say, "Fortunate are you, O years of my old age, for you will atone for the years of my youth"—these [who say this song] are the penitents [T. Suk. 4:2].**

[II.A] Hillel the Elder: When he would see people acting arrogantly, would say to them, "If I am here, who is here?"

[B]   "Does [God] need their praise? And is it not written, 'A stream of fire issued and came forth from before him; a thousand thousands served him, and ten thousand times ten thousand stood before him; the court sat in judgement, and the books were opened'" (Dan. 7:10).

[C]   When he would see people acting modestly, he would say to them, "If we are not here, who is here? For even though [God] has before him any number of those who praise him, still, precious to him is the praise coming from Israel more than anything else.

[D]   "What is the scriptural basis for this statement? '[Now these are the last words of David: The oracle of David, the son of Jesse, the oracle of the man who was raised on high, the anointed of the God of Jacob,] the sweet-psalmist of Israel' (2 Sam. 23:1).

[E]   "'. . . enthroned [55c] on the praises of Israel'" (Ps. 22:4).

[III.A] [As to the dancing,] Ben Yehosedeq was praised because of his jumping about.

[B]   **M'SH B: Rabban Simeon b. Gamaliel danced with eight flaming torches, and not one of them fell to the ground.**

[C]   **Now when he would prostrate himself, he would put his finger on the ground, bow low, kiss [the ground], and forthwith straighten up [T. Suk. 4:4].**

[**IV.**A]   What is bowing and what is kneeling?

[B]   R. Hiyya the Elder demonstrated an act of bowing before Rabbi, and he was lamed and healed.

[C]   Levi bar Sisi demonstrated an act of kneeling before Rabbi, and he was lamed but not healed.

[**V.**A]   "And David returned to bless his household. But Michal the daughter of Saul came out to meet David, [and said, 'How the king of Israel honored himself today, uncovering himself today before the eyes of his servants' maids, as one of the vulgar fellows shamelessly uncovers himself!']" (2 Sam. 6:20).

[B]   What is the meaning of "one of the vulgar fellows"?

[C]   Said R. Abba bar Kahana, "The most vulgar of them all—this is a dancer!"

[D]   She said to him, "Today the glory of father's house was revealed."

[E]   They said about Saul's house that [they were so modest] that their heel and their toe never saw [their privy parts].

[F]   This is in line with that which is written, "And he came to the sheepfolds [by the way, where there was a cave; and Saul went in to relieve himself]" (1 Sam. 24:3).

[G]   R. Abun in the name of R. Eleazar: "It was a sheepfold within yet another sheepfold."

[H]   "And Saul went in to relieve himself: ["cover his feet"]: [David] saw him lower his garments slightly and excrete slightly [as needed].

[I]   [David] said, "How can anyone lay a hand on such a righteous body!"

[J]   This is in line with that which he said to him, "Lo, this day your eyes have seen how the Lord gave you today into my hand in the cave; and some bade me kill you, but *it* spared you" (1 Sam. 24:10).

[K]   It is not written, "*I* spared you," but "*It* spared you"—that is, "Your own modesty is what spared you."

[L]   "And David said to Michal, 'It was before the Lord, who chose me above your father, and above all his house, to appoint me as prince over Israel, the people of the Lord—and I will make merry before the Lord. I will make myself yet more contemptible than this, and I will be abased in your eyes; but by the maids of whom you have spoken, by them I shall be held in honor'" (2 Sam. 6:21–22).

[M]   For they are not handmaidens, but mothers.

[N]   And how was Michal punished? "And Michal the daughter of Saul had no child [to the day of her death]" (2 Sam. 6:23).

[O]   And is it now not written, ". . . and the sixth was Ithream of Eglah, David's wife" (2 Sam. 3:5)?

[P]   She lowed like a cow (Eglah) and expired [giving birth on the day of her death].

Unit **I** complements M. 5:4B by specifying the songs the various singers sang. Why unit **II** is included I do not know; T.'s complement likewise contains a collection of Hillel materials. Units **III** and **IV** provide materials on dancing and juggling, an anthology on M.'s principal theme. Unit **V** is included as a disquisition on a verse of Scripture also pertinent to dancing.

5:5

[A]   *And two priests stood at the upper gate which goes down from the Israelites' court to the women's court, with two trumpets in their hands.*

[B]   *[When] the cock crowed, they sounded a sustained, a quavering, and a sustained note on the shofar.*

[C]   *[When] they got to the tenth step, they sounded a sustained, a quavering, and a sustained blast on the shofar.*

[D]   *[When] they reached the courtyard, they sounded a sustained, a quavering, and a sustained blast on the shofar.*

[E]   *They went on sounding the shofar in a sustained blast until they reached the gate which leads out to the east.*

[F]   *[When] they reached the gate which leads out to the east, they sounded a sustained, a quavering, and a sustained blast on the shofar.*

[G]   *[When] they reached the gate which goes out toward the east, they turned around toward the west,*

[H]   *and they said, "Our fathers who were in this place 'turned with their backs toward the Temple of the Lord and their faces toward the east, and they bowed down to the sun toward the east' (Ezek. 8:16).*

[I]   *"But as to us, our eyes are to the Lord."*

[J]   *R. Judah says, "They said it a second time, 'We belong to the Lord, our eyes are toward the Lord.'"*

[I.A]   [As to M. 5:5B, *When the cock crowed,*] Rab interpreted before the members of the house of R. Shiloh, "The cock crowed," as "The crier proclaimed."

[B]   They said to him, "[does it not mean,] 'The cock (GBR) crowed'?"

[C]   He said to them, "And lo, we have learned the language, 'Son of man (GBR) (M. Sheq. 5:1).' Can you claim that this means, 'Son of a chicken'?"

[II.A]   R. Jeremiah asked, "[With reference to the tenth step, M. 5:5C,] is this the tenth from the top, or the tenth from the bottom?"

[III.A]   Said R. Hiyya bar Ba, "It is not written here [at Ezek. 8:16], 'They made an act of prostration' [one time], but rather, 'They made two acts of prostration' [twice]. For they prostrated themselves both to the sun and to the Temple."

[B]   Said R. Abba bar Kana, "'For my people have committed two evils: they have forsaken me, the fountain of living waters, and hewed out cisterns for themselves, broken cisterns, that can hold no water' (Jer. 2:13).

[C]   "And is it so that [only] two evils did my people commit? And lo, he forgave a thousand.

[D]   "But [the two evils here are that they] prostrated themselves to the sun and also prostrated themselves to the Temple [at once, that is, with their faces to the sun and their backsides to the Temple]."

The Talmud takes up and interprets or amplifies several of the Mishnah's components.

5:6

[A]   *They sound no fewer than twenty-one notes in the Temple, and they do not sound more than forty-eight.*

[B]   *Every day there were there twenty-one blasts on the* shofar:

[C]   *three at the opening of the gates, nine at the offering of the daily whole-offering of the morning, and nine at the offering of the daily whole-offering of the evening.*

[D]   *And on days on which an additional offering is made, they would add nine more.*

[E]   *And on the eve of the Sabbath they would add six more:*

[F]   *three to make people stop working, and three to mark the border between the holy day and the ordinary day.*

[G]   *On the eve of the Sabbath which came during the Festival there were forty-eight in all:*

[H]   *three for the opening of the gates, three for the upper gate and three for the lower gate, three for the drawing of the water, three for the pouring of the water on the altar, nine for the offering of the daily whole-offering in the morning, nine for the offering of the daily whole-offering of the evening, nine for the additional offerings, three to make the people stop work, and three to mark the border between the holy day and the ordinary day.*

[I.A]   It has been taught [as against M. 5:6A]: There were no fewer than seven and no more than sixteen.

[B]   The Tanna [responsible for I.A] counts the three sounds [long, quavering, and long] as a single note,

[C]   while the Tanna [responsible for M. 5:6A] counts them individually [one by one].

[D]   [As to the nine for the daily whole-offering, M. 5:6C,] you turn out to have three for each time they bowed their heads [during that rite].

[E]   R. Judah says, "There are three for each paragraph [of the psalms read at that time]."

[F]   And lo, it has been taught: Nine [Better: *Three*] *when they got to the tenth step [M. 5:5C].* So there are other blasts on the horn [besides those listed here].

[G]   He who maintains that they sounded the ram's horn at the altar does not concur that they sounded it at the tenth step,

[H]   while he who holds that they sounded it at the tenth step does not maintain that they sounded it at the altar.

[II.A]   ["With respect to M. 5:6H, *Three for the drawing of the water,*"] said R. Zeirah, "that is to say that they sounded the horn only at the water-libation [but not for the actual drawing of the water for that purpose].

[B]   "For if [to the contrary] you wish to maintain that they did so for the drawing of the water as well as for the actual water-libation, then the passage should state, 'Three for drawing the water for the day, and three for drawing the water for the next day,' [since, as we recall, the water was drawn for the libation on the preceding day]. [Hence there are two water-rites on a given day, one for drawing the water for the next day, the other for the pouring out of the water for the day in question.]"

[III.A]   [As to M. 5:6D, nine for the Additional Offering:] Are these the only ones? You have other [Additional Offerings, on certain occasions, while the Mishnah speaks of only one such offering].

[B]   [That is,] there should be nine for the Additional Offering of the Sabbath, and nine for the Additional Offering of the New Moon [that coincides with the Sabbath], and nine for the Additional Offering of the festival offering of the New Year.

[C]   But does the passage conform to the view of him who said, "'[And the sons of Aaron, the priests,] shall blow trumpets. [The trumpets shall be to you for a perpetual statute throughout your generations]' (Num. 10:8). [This means that] they sound the trumpet in accord with the number of Additional Offerings"?

[D]   Rabbis of Caesarea in the name of R. Jacob bar Aha, "And even in accord with the view of him who said, '"they shall blow the trumpets" [means that] they sound the trumpet in accord with the number of Additional Offerings,' [his meaning is that] they sound the trumpet for Additional Offerings, but they do not add soundings of the trumpet to accord with the number of separate and distinct Additional Offerings." [For the readings translated here, compare PM and QH. The entire discussion takes for granted materials not in Y. but at B. Suk. 54a.]

[IV.A]   R. Hiyya bar Ba said, "The lyre is the same as the lute, except that there are more strings in the one [lyre = *nebel*] than in the other."

[B]   Said R. Hiyya b. Aba, "Why is it called a lyre (*nebel*)? Because [through the beauty of its sounds] it shames many other kinds of musical instruments [that cannot make such beautiful sounds]."

[C]   R. Hunah in the name of R. Joseph: "Because of hide, that is not worked, and because of its extra strings, it shames any number of other musical instruments."

[D]   R. Simeon b. Laqish said, "An organ is a water-organ."

[E]   Rabban Simeon b. Gamaliel taught, "There was no water-organ in Jerusalem, because it spoils the sweetness [of the singing]."

[F]   [What follows is in T.'s version:] **The pipe which was in the sanctuary was made of reed, and it came down from the time of Moses. One time they covered it with gold, and its sound was not so pleasant as it had been. They removed the plate, and its sound again became pleasant as it had been [Y.: It was damaged and they repaired it, but its sound. . . . They removed the damaged. . . . and its sound. . . .]**

[G]   **A cymbal which was in the sanctuary was made of copper, and it came down from the time of Moses. It was damaged. [Y. lacks:] Sages sent and imported craftsmen from Alexandria, and [Y. resumes:] they fixed it. But its sound was not so pleasant as it had been [T. Ar. 2:3]. [Y. adds: They removed (the place which had been damaged) and it was restored to its original condition.]**

[H]   **There was a mortar which was in the sanctuary, made of bronze. And it came from the time of Moses. It was damaged. [Y. lacks:] Sages sent and imported craftsmen from Alexandria, and [Y. resumes:] they repaired it. But it was not as it should be. They removed the place which had been damaged. It was restored to its original condition [T. Ar. 2:4].**

[I]   **There are two utensils which were damaged in the time of the first Temple and were not repaired, and concerning them, it** says, "They were of burnished brass" (1 Kings 7:45), and concerning them it says, "And two vessels of fine, bright brass, [55d] precious as gold" (Ezra 8:27). This teaches that it was twice as lovely as gold [T. Ar. 2:5].

[J] There are two Amoras. One says, "One of them was twice as lovely as gold."

[K] The other says, "Both of them were twice as lovely as gold."

[L] It has been taught: **Rabban Simeon b. Gamaliel says, "Siloam gushed forth water through a hole the size of an *issar*. They said, 'Let us make it wider, so that water will gush forth more abundantly from it.' So they widened it. But its water became sparse. They stopped it up, and it returned to its original condition"** [T. Ar. 2:6].

[M] As to the musical instrument called the *magrepah:*

[N] Rab and Samuel: One said, "It has ten openings. Each one produced a hundred notes."

[O] The other said, "It had a hundred openings. Each one produced ten notes."

[P] In the view of both parties, it produced a thousand notes.

[V.A] [When the New Moon coincides with the Sabbath,] as to the Additional Offerings of the Sabbath and of the New Moon, which is offered first [and so takes precedence]?

[B] R. Jeremiah contemplated ruling, "When the Additional Offerings of the Sabbath and the Additional Offerings of the New Moon coincide, the Additional Offerings of the New Moon take precedence."

[C] Support for the position of R. Jeremiah derives from the following: When there is the Psalm for the Sabbath and the Psalm for the New Moon, the Psalm for the New Moon takes precedence.

[D] Said R. Yose, "That case is different. For R. Hiyya said in the name of R. Yohanan, 'It is in order to publicize the matter and to make known that it is the New Moon.

[E] "'What should he do? He should slaughter the Additional Offering for the Sabbath and say in that regard the Psalm for the New Moon.'

[F]   "But here, [Yose said, rejecting **V.B–C,**] by contrast, where there are the Additional Offerings of the Sabbath and the Additional Offerings of the New Moon [to be dealt with], the Additional Offerings of the Sabbath take precedence.

[G]   "It is on the principle that whatever is more regular than its fellow takes precedence over its fellow."

Units **I** and **II** go over the number of times the ram's horn is sounded during the Temple rites. The translation-interpretation of unit **III** is somewhat conjectural. A glance at M. Ar. 2:3A, which is the same as M. 5:6A, explains the insertion of unit **IV,** which serves M. Ar. 2:3. I assume that if there were a Talmud of the Land of Israel to serve M. Ar. 2:3, it would then include units **I–III** before us. Unit **V** raises a secondary question on the coincidence of the Sabbath and the New Moon, provoked by M. 5:6G I assume.

5:7

[A]   *On the first festival day of the Festival there were there thirteen bullocks, two rams, and one goat [Num. 29:13, 16].*

[B]   *There remained fourteen lambs for the eight priestly watches.*

[C]   *On the first day, six offer two each, and the remaining two, one each.*

[D]   *On the second day, five offer two each, and the rest, one each.*

[E]   *On the third day, four offer two each, and the rest, one each.*

[F]   *On the fourth day, three offer two each, and the rest offer one each.*

[G]   *On the fifth day, two offer two each, and the rest offer one each.*

[H]   *On the sixth day, one offers two, and the rest offer one each.*

[I]   *On the seventh, all of them are equal.*

[J]   *On the eighth, they go back to drawing lots, as on the [other] festivals.*

[K]   *They ruled: Whoever offered a bullock one day should not offer one the next day.*

[L]   *But they offer them in rotation.*

[I.A]   It has been taught: **All the priestly courses repeat the offering of a bullock during the seven days of the Festival a second and a third time, except for the last two, which repeat but do not do it a third time in the case of the bullocks** [cf. **M. 5:7K–L**] **[T. Suk. 4:15A].**

[B]   R. Eleazar asked, "What is the law as to beginning with them for the next festival?"

[C]   Said R. Yose, "The Mishnah has made that point: *On the eighth they go back to drawing lots, as on the other festivals [M. 5:7J].*"

[D]   No, it was necessary to raise this question in accord with that which was taught by R. Nathan.

[E]   For R. Nathan taught, "On the eighth day there was no drawing of lots."

[F]   So in accord with the position of R. Nathan, what is the law as to beginning with them for the next festival?

[G]   Said R. Yohanan,

[H]   And so too has it been taught: **Now the last day of the Festival had a drawing of lots unto itself, a time unto itself, a festival unto itself, an offering unto itself, a song unto itself, a blessing unto itself. [Thus each festival is treated as a separate entity, and there is no transfer of rights for the priestly watches from one festival to the next] [T. Suk. 4:17A].**

[I]   As to the festival unto itself [meaning, a blessing framed in terms of that festival in particular, e.g., ". . . who has kept us in life . . .":] this is in line with what R. Abin said in the name of R. Aha, "In the case of all of the seven other [days of Tabernacles, Num. 29:12–34 persistently use the conjunction, *and*, e.g., *And* on the second day,] while in regard to the eighth day, it says only, 'On the eighth day' (Num. 29:35). This serves to teach you that the eighth day of Solemn Assembly is a festival unto itself."

[J]   As to the lottery [by itself]:

[K]   Said R. Yose, "The Mishnah has made that point: *On the eighth they go back to drawing lots, as on the other festivals [M. 5:7J].*"

[L]   As to the blessing:

[M]   Said R. Ila, "One has to say, 'Who has kept us in life and sustained us and brought us to this time.'"

[N]   As to an offering:

[O]   It is a bullock and a ram.

We deal with the priests' assignments in offering up the various public offerings for the Festival. There were twenty-four priestly watches, all of them allowed to share in the sacrifices. Sixteen of these were occupied with the sixteen beasts, M. 5:7A. Eight were left over for turns on the remainder of the Festival, B. C–I then spell out the consequences. On the first day six of the eight watches offer two sacrifices apiece, and two watches offer one, and so on down, in line with Num. 29:17–32. The point of K–L is that twenty-two priestly watches offer bullocks three times and two have only two turns. The reference, M. 5:7J, to other festivals, then generates the inclusion of M. 5:8. The Talmud provides a systematic account of Tosefta's complement to the Mishnah. It indicates that Nathan, I.D–E, does not concur with M. Then, I.F–O, it presents an account of the separate status of the eighth day of assembly, in line with M. 5:7J.

5:8

[A]   *Three times a year all the priestly watches shared equally in the offerings of the feasts and in the division of the Show Bread.*

[B]   *At Pentecost they would say to him, "Here you have unleavened bread, here is leavened bread for you."*

[C]   *The priestly watch whose time of service is scheduled [for that week] is the one which offers the daily whole-offerings, the offerings brought by reason of vows and freewill offerings, and the other public offerings.*

[D]   *And it offers everything.*

[E]   *On the festival day which comes next to a Sabbath, whether before or after it, all of the priestly watches were equal in the division of the Show Bread.*

[F]   *[If] a day intervened [between a festival day and a Sabbath], the priestly watch which was scheduled for that time took ten loaves, and the one that stayed back [in the Temple] took two.*

[G]   *And on all other days of the year, the entering priestly watch took six, and the one going off duty took six.*

[H]   *R. Judah says, "The one coming on duty takes seven, and the one going off duty takes five."*

[I]   *The ones going on duty divide at the north, and the ones going off duty divide at the south.*

[J]   *[The priestly watch of] Bilgah always divided it in the south, and their ring was fixed, and their wall-niche was blocked up.*

[I.A]   [Proving that all the priestly watches share equally on the festivals,] it is written, "They shall have portion to portion to eat" (Deut. 18 : 8).

[B]   Is it possible that the same rule applies on all the other days of the year?

[C]   Scripture says, "Besides what he receives from the sale of his patrimony" (Deut 18 : 8).

[D]   This is exclusive of what the fathers have sold to the sons, thus: "You have your week, and I have my week."

[II.A]   *At Pentecost they would say to him, "Here you have unleavened bread, here is leavened bread for you" [M. 5 : 8B]:*

[B]   There is a Tanna who reverses the order and repeats the tradition as follows: "Here is leavened bread for you, here is unleavened bread for you."

[C]   He who teaches [first], "Here is unleavened bread for you" [gives it precedence] because it is more desirable.

[D]   He who teaches [first], "Here is leavened bread for you" [gives it precedence] because it is more regular[ly distributed to the priests than unleavened bread].

[III.A]   Said R. Levi, "[At the outset, before the division of the priestly emoluments,] all the watches are located in the south [of the altar, and then the officiating watch goes to the north, so as to distinguish it from the watch whose term of service has ended]."

[B]   Said R. Yose, "The Mishnah contains the same implication: *If a day intervened between [a festival day and a Sabbath] [M. 5 : 8F].* [That is, the two watches were located in a single direction vis-à-vis the altar, then one group would be set off from the other and receive its distinct emolument.]"

[C]   R. Judah b. Titus in the name of R. Aha, "The Scripture sup-
ports the view of that Tanna: 'Now then, what have you in hand?
Give me five loaves of bread or whatever is here' (1 Sam. 21:4).
Now Ahimelech [who figures in this story] was a member of the
outgoing priestly watch. [How David knew that Ahimelech had
five loaves is explained by PM.]"

[IV.A]   *The ones going on duty divide at the north, and the ones going
off duty divide at the south [M. 5:8/I].*

[B]   Said R. Hananiah, son of R. Hillel, "[the ones coming in are
given the place of honor, at the north of the altar] so as to pay
respect to the ones who are coming on duty."

[C]   Said R. Yose b. R. Bun, "It is not for this reason. But it is on
account of what we have learned: *All those who enter the Temple
mount enter at the right, go around, and leave at the left [M.
Mid. 2:2A]. [If one goes right, he hits the northern side of the
altar first.]"*

[V.A]   *[The priestly watch of] Bilgah always divided it in the south,
and their ring was fixed, and their wall-niche was blocked up
[M. 5:8J]:*

[B]   [In T.'s version:] **because of Miriam, daughter of Bilgah, who
apostasized.**

[C]   **She went off and married an officer of the Greek royal house.**

[D]   **And when the gentiles went into the sanctuary, she came
along and stamped on the top of the altar, screaming at it,
"Wolf, wolf! You have wiped out the fortune of Israel, and
you [still] did not then stand up for them in the time of their
trouble!"**

[E]   **And some say it was because [the priestly watch of Bilgah]
delayed in observing its priestly watch.**

[F]   **So the watch of Yeshebab went in and served [Y.: as high
priest] in its stead.**

[G]   **Therefore Bilgah always appears to be among the outgoing
priestly watches [at the south], and Yeshebab always appears
to be among the incoming priestly watches [at the north].**

[H]   **[Y. omits:] Neighbors of the wicked normally receive no
reward,**

[I]   **except for Yeshebab,**

[J]   **neighbor to Bilgah, who received a reward [T. Suk. 4:28].**

[K]   And why not remove the priestly watch of Bilgah entirely?

[L]   You cannot do so, for R. Simon said in the name of R. Joshua b. Levi, "It is difficult for the Omnipresent totally to uproot a genealogical chain from its rightful place."

[M]   Then why not make the priestly watches twenty-three [instead of twenty-four, dividing this watch among the others, rather than recognizing it as a watch by itself]?

[N]   You cannot do so, for it is written, "[All these, who were chosen as gatekeepers at the thresholds, were two hundred and twelve. They were enrolled by genealogies in their villages.] David and Samuel the seer established them in their office of trust" (1 Chron. 9:22).

[O]   It was an act of skilled work.

[P]   Great skill was displayed there, for one watch does not take a second portion in the fields of possession [sold by the original family during the years preceding the Jubilee and not redeemed by them, such fields then falling to the ownership of the priest-hood and being divided among the watches], until its fellow-watch has taken its share.

[Q]   Said R. Abbahu, "[It is as if to say,] 'I gave thought to them to see that one priestly watch does not take a second share among the fields of possession until its fellow takes one first.'"

[VI.A]   *And their ring was fixed [M. 5:8J]:*

[B]   R. Ba in the name of R. Judah: "They made rings for them-selves, broad at the top and narrow at the bottom."

[VII.A]   *And their wall-niche was blocked up [M. 5:8J]:*

[B]   This was so that they would not use the space for their knives.

[C]   It is in line with that which we have learned there: *It was called the place of the room of the slaughter-knives, for there did they put away the knives [M. Mid. 4:7F].*

We turn to the shares of the priestly watches on other festivals. The principal interest is in the division of the Show Bread, M. 5:8A–B, E, F–J. The Show Bread is removed from the table and replaced on the Sabbath. What is taken away is given out to the priests. Now, if all the priests are available, who gets it? All divide it, if all are present, M. 5:8E. But if there is an intervening day, e.g., if the festival fell on Thursday, then the priestly watch in charge for the following Sabbath took ten loaves. What about the watch which served the preceding week but remained in the Temple over the Sabbath, since it came so close to the festival? That watch took two. Unit **I** provides a scriptural basis for M. 5:8A. Unit **II** examines the traditions on M.'s formulation. Unit **III** provides an exegesis for M. 5:8F, as indicated. Unit **IV** explains M.'s rule. Unit **V** cites T.'s complement to M.'s statement. Units **VI** and **VII** cite and gloss M. So in all the Talmud stays close to the labor of explaining the statements and foundations of the Mishnah's rules.

Abbreviations, Bibliography, and Glossary

Ar.: Arakhin

b.: *Babli,* Babylonian Talmud; *ben,* "son of"

B.B.: Baba Batra

B.M.: Baba Mesia

B.Q.: Baba Qama

B. Suk.: Babylonian Talmud Tractate Sukkah

Bet hashshoebah: A festival at the end of the Festival of Tabernacles

Chron.: Chronicles

Dem.: Demai, produce about which there is a doubt whether or not the required heave-offering and tithes were removed

Deut.: Deuteronomy

Ephah: A measure of dry volume

Er.: Erubin

Etrog: A citron, carried on the Festival of Booths as the "fruit of goodly trees," mentioned at Lev. 23:40

Ex.: Exodus

Gen.: Genesis

Git.: Gittin

Hag.: Hagigah

Hallel: A portion of the liturgy, consisting of Psalms 113–18, recited on festivals and new moons

hin: A measure of liquid volume

Hor.: Horayot

Kel.: Kelim

Ket.: Ketubot

Kil.: Kilayim

L[eiden MS]: *The Palestinian Talmud. Leiden MS. Cod Scal. 3. A facsimile of the original manuscript.* With introduction by Saul Lieberman. 4 vols. Jerusalem: Kedem Publishing, 1970

Lev.: Leviticus

Log: One seventy-second of an *ephah*

Lulab: The branches of palm, myrtle, and willow that are bound together and carried along with the *etrog* on the Festival of Booths (see Lev. 23:40)

M.: Mishnah

M.S.: Maasar Sheni

Mezuzah: A strip of parchment inscribed with Deut. 6:4–9 and

11:18–21. In accordance with Deut. 6:9 it is fastened to the doorpost of an Israelite's house (pl.: *mezuzot*)

Mid.: Middot

MꞋSH B (W): A formulaic phrase used to introduce a legal precedent

Naz.: Nazir

PM: Pené Moshe: Moses Margolies (d. 1780). *Pene Moshe.* Amsterdam: 1754; Leghorn: 1770. Reprinted in the Yerushalmi Talmud

Par.: Parah

Pe.: Peah

Pes.: Pesahim

Prov.: Proverbs

Ps.: Psalms

QH: Qorban Ha Edah

Qid.: Qiddushin

Qoh.: Qohelet [= Ecclesiastes]

R.: Rabbi

Seah: One-third of an *ephah*

Shab.: Shabbat

Sheb.: Shebiit

Shebu.: Shebuot

Shofar: A ram's horn, blown on set occasions in Temple and synagogue worship

Suk.: Sukkah

Sukkah: A temporary dwelling ("booth") in which Israelites live during the Festival of Tabernacles, in fulfillment of Lev. 23: 34–36, 39–43

T.: Tosefta

Tam.: Tamid

Tebul yom: A person who has immersed in a ritual bath and awaits the setting of the sun, which marks the completion of the process of purification

Ter.: Terumot

Ulam: Temple area

Y.: Yerushalmi—Talmud of the Land of Israel

V: *Talmud Yerushalmi . . . Venezia* (*editio princeps* printed by Daniel Bomberg 1523–24; repr. without date or place)

Index of Biblical and Talmudic References

Arthur W. Woodman

General Index

Arthur W. Woodman

Abba bar Hanah: *lulab* and *etrog*, 84; physical requirements of *sukkah*, 44

Abba bar Kahana, rites of *sukkot*, 104, 125, 127

Abba of Kipa, *lulab* and *etrog*, 84

Abba Saul: *lulab* and *etrog*, 71; rites of *sukkot*, 93

Abbahu: *lulab* and *etrog*, 84; physical requirements of *sukkah*, 10, 15, 17, 23, 39; rites of *sukkot*, 99, 111; *sukkot*-offering, Show Bread, 137

Abedimi of Haifa, physical requirements of *sukkah*, 22

Abin: *lulab* and *etrog*, 68; physical requirements of *sukkah*, 8, 34; rites of *sukkot*, 104; *sukkot*-offering, Show Bread, 133

Abina: *lulab* and *etrog*, 68; rites of *sukkot*, 101, 113

Abodemi, rites of *sukkot*, 104

Abona, dwelling in *sukkah*, 58

Abun: dwelling in *sukkah*, 61; *lulab* and *etrog*, 90; rites of *sukkot*, 125

Aha: dwelling in *sukkah*, 59–60; *lulab* and *etrog*, 82; physical requirements of *sukkah*, 7, 10, 50, 52–53; rites of *sukkot*, 101, 104, 112–13; *sukkot*-offering, Show Bread, 133, 136

Ahi, rites of *sukkot*, 97

Aibu bar Nigri: dwelling in *sukkah*, 60–61; rites of *sukkot*, 99

Aqiba: *lulab* and *etrog*, 68, 72, 79–81; physical requirements of *sukkah*, 50, 54; rites of *sukkot*, 94, 100, 106–7

Ba: physical requirements of *sukkah*, 11, 20, 32–33, 43, 48; rites of *sukkot*, 94, 102–3; *sukkot*-offering, Show Bread, 137

Ba bar Mamel: *lulab* and *etrog*, 73; physical requirements of *sukkah*, 13–14, 16, 23, 39; rites of *sukkot*, 115

Ba Sarongayyah, rites of *sukkot*, 99

Ba bar Zabeda: dwelling in *sukkah*, 55; rites of *sukkot*, 94

Bar Qappara: dwelling in *sukkah*, 59; physical requirements of *sukkah*, 8; rites of *sukkot*, 98, 100, 121

Benjamin bar Levi, rites of *sukkot*, 117

Berekhian: dwelling in *sukkah*, 58; rites of *sukkot*, 99–100

Bibi, physical requirements of *sukkah*, 32

Bun, physical requirements of *sukkah*, 23, 37

Bun bar Hiyya, physical requirements of *sukkah*, 24

Dosa, rites of *sukkot*, 96–98

Eleazar: dwelling in *sukkah*, 55–56; *lulab* and *etrog*, 66, 78, 84; rites of *sukkot*, 97, 102–3, 106, 125; *sukkot*-offering, Show Bread, 133

Eleazar b. Azariah, physical requirements of *sukkah*, 50

Eleazar b. Diglai, rites of *sukkot*, 123

Eleazar b. Parta, *lulab* and *etrog*, 85

Eleazar b. Sadog, rites of *sukkot*, 108

Eliezer: dwelling in *sukkah*, 57–61, 64; *lulab* and *etrog*, 78; physical requirements of *sukkah*, 43–46; rites of *sukkot*, 98–100